The Everyday Healthy

THE EVERYDAY HEALTHY *Vegetarian*

DELICIOUS MEALS FROM THE INDIAN KITCHEN

NANDITA IYER

hachette INDIA

First published in 2017 by Hachette India
(Registered name: Hachette Book Publishing India Pvt. Ltd)
An Hachette UK company
www.hachetteindia.com

1

Photograph on pages vi, xix courtesy Bharath Moro

All nutritional information courtesy HealthifyMe.

Book design by Tara Upadhyay
Illustrations by Pia Hazarika

ISBN 978-93-5009-827-1

Hachette Book Publishing India Pvt. Ltd
4th & 5th Floors, Corporate Centre,
Plot No. 94, Sector 44, Gurugram - 122003, India

Typeset by Manmohan Kumar, Delhi
Printed and bound in India
by Manipal Technologies Limited, Manipal

To my family

M.K. INDUS

Contents

GOOD CARBS

PROTEIN PUNCH

The Birth of This Book

Fifteen years ago, for a brief period of time, I lived in Shivaji Park, Mumbai, in a shared paying-guest accommodation with four other women. A terrace converted into a large hall-like room with five single beds, five small steel almirahs and a bathroom – it was the most basic of spaces to live in. A *cudappah* (stone) slab in one corner of the room with a two-burner gas stove and a couple of stone shelves underneath it constituted the kitchen. The five of us took turns cooking, and the constraints of space, appliances and ingredients ensured that the food was utterly basic – essentially dal-rice, khichdi, poha or anything else that could be made in a small pressure cooker and/or a kadhai. My studies and job left me with no time or energy to experiment in the kitchen, after all.

During that phase in my life, there was neither the time nor the wherewithal to cook anything beyond the basics. Perhaps to compensate for this – and to nurture my passion for food – I started scribbling down recipes or ideas for dishes in the form of a makeshift cookbook. However, these armchair cooking escapades in a foolscap notebook seemed silly even to me.

After I got married, I moved to the United States and my books, along with other sundry items, were packed in cartons, left at my parents' home in Mumbai, and consequently forgotten. This move brought food back into my life, and I started cooking a great deal more. Thankfully, my husband was a fuss-free eater and welcomed my culinary experiments with enthusiasm. His encouragement pushed me to let loose my creativity in the kitchen and, in March 2006, I started my food blog at a time when 'food blog' wasn't even a legitimate term.

The blog, which I named *Saffron Trail,* began as a place where I could record the recipes I had created on an impulse and tried out on my husband. Given my medical degree and study of nutrition, the food I prepared always followed the basic principles of healthy eating, but did not compromise on taste. Over the years, my focus shifted to recipes that would benefit people who wanted to lead a healthier lifestyle. My attention to diabetic-friendly recipes, quick weeknight dinners for working professionals, incorporating superfoods into one's diet, etc., received a lot of positive feedback from readers. *Saffron Trail* slowly grew in terms of both content and audience, and today has over 700 recipes with a wonderful and loyal reader base that keeps encouraging me to invent, cook and share more of my cooking.

When I shared the news of signing a book deal with my Amma, she unexpectedly brought up the forgotten notebook of recipes I had left with her. 'I saw that notebook with your handwritten recipes among your packed things years ago. I'm proud that your dream has turned into reality,' she said. Her gentle praise brought back memories of the girl who had dreamt of writing a cookbook even when she had a barely-functional kitchen.

I strongly believe that every little dream, even those that are buried deep within our subconscious, become building blocks for our future. This book is proof of that.

What This Book Will Do for You

This book aims to guide you in the concepts of healthy cooking and eating, to help you appreciate the versatility of easily available Indian ingredients and superfoods that can be incorporated in your diet. Healthy food does not have to be tasteless or break-the-bank expensive. It is also not meant to be time-consuming. This book is not about fancy recipes or haute cuisine; it's about using everyday ingredients to create simple meals, but with a healthy twist. Most of these recipes will have you cooking from scratch, but that does not mean you will spend the better part of your day in the kitchen. The only meals I cook are the ones that do not take more than 30 minutes, so you can trust me not to subject you to arduous cooking procedures.

Within these pages, you will find interesting meal combinations that are also nutritionally balanced. For example, a boiled potato, roti and rice are all carbohydrates. Dal, sprouts, eggs, beans, cheese, tofu, etc. are all protein-rich foods. What nutrition elements we choose to combine for a balanced meal, however, is totally up to us – put together potatoes, beans/eggs and vegetables in a bowl and you have a balanced meal with carbs, proteins, fats, vitamins and minerals.

Keeping the nutrient groups in mind, I have divided the book into four sections, each of which contains recipes that can be combined with recipes in other sections to prepare a balanced meal.

The **Good Carbs** section includes hearty recipes featuring starchy vegetables such as potatoes and sweet potatoes, and grains like millet, barley, unprocessed rice, oats and more.

The **Eat the Rainbow** section shows you interesting ways to use the same old vegetables and fruits, including a host of satisfying salads with bright flavours that use locally-available ingredients and will make you fall in love with the salad-a-day concept.

The **Protein Punch** section takes care of the hardest-to-incorporate nutrients in a vegetarian diet. Armed with the right knowledge, it is easy for vegetarians to get the required quantity of protein in their daily diet. Use the recipes from this section to amp up your protein intake. Here, you will find some traditional ingredients used in modern ways, for example, black-eyed peas (lobia) in a salad or a burger. For those of you who eat eggs, I have included a few egg-based recipes, though I have tried to give egg-replacement ideas for some of them.

The **Healthy Fats** section will help you incorporate good fats in your diet – fats that are vital for the functioning of the brain and the reproductive system as well as for absorbing fat-soluble vitamins. In this section you will find recipes featuring seeds, nuts, avocado and healthy cold-pressed oils. Some salad dressings that are rich in healthy fats are included as a part of salad recipes in the 'Eat the Rainbow' section.

Simplicity is the backbone of this book. The recipes have a reasonably short list of ingredients and employ cooking techniques that will appeal even to beginners in the kitchen. Choosing minimum ingredients with maximum flavour is the way I like to cook and the recipes you will find here follow that philosophy. Furthermore, while most recipes are written for singles, couples and small families (two to four people), you can easily double or triple the quantities to serve larger families or a group of friends.

At the back of the book, you will find two indices – one based on ingredients and the other on dietary constraints. So whether you are diabetic or a vegan or maintain a gluten-free diet, or simply want to know which recipes use superfoods in order to incorporate them in your diet, use the dietary index to know which recipes from the book will work for you.

You will also find a sample weekly menu at the end of the book – use this to start your journey towards healthy eating and then mix and match meals as you wish! Soon, you will be able to use the variations given in some of the recipes along with your own staple favourites to prepare your own weekly menu plans. This not only makes you a more organized cook, but you also save on multiple trips to the supermarket or hours spent on an online shopping app. To make healthy eating a part of your lifestyle it is important to plan out every last detail. Once you have decided what you are going to cook for the whole week, you will find that it's quite hard to derail your well-made plans.

While many of the recipes are inspired by traditional Indian cuisine, you will find global influences in here too. This will break the monotony in your daily meals and make healthy eating exciting.

Keeping the cooking simple and fast, while harnessing the nourishing properties of healthy ingredients, this book attempts to give you recipes for food that is quick to prepare and delicious to eat. Whether you are a busy professional with a nine-to-five job or a parent (or both!), I want this to be your go-to book for when you want to cook healthy.

My Kitchen

My kitchen is my happy place; sun-dappled in the early hours of the day, mellowing as the day progresses. My day starts here with a cup of ginger tea as I mull over what to cook for breakfast, lunch and dinner. No surprises there, right?

Having said that, I am not as neat and organized in the kitchen department as I would like to be. While I am particular about cleanliness, having a completely clutter-free counter is beyond me. The microwave oven, the knife block, the coffee filter and other regulars like the oil basket and the masala *dabba* are permanent residents of the countertop. Even though there are enough cabinets in my kitchen to hold most of the provisions, I do wish I had a separate alcove for a pantry, decked up with fairy lights, a la Nigella Lawson. I stock some of the flours, grains and nuts in the refrigerator, just to make them last a little longer.

Once or twice a week, I shop for fresh produce, sometimes resorting to the ease of online shopping and at other times experiencing the joy of shopping in supermarkets (though I find no joy in standing in the endless billing queues!). Whenever I am in Mumbai, I make it a point to visit the open markets. The familiar sharp fragrance from trucks full of fresh coriander, the sheer abundance of seasonal vegetables and the general cacophony in the atmosphere are a delight to my senses.

My refrigerator is stocked depending on what I plan to cook that week. Tomatoes, avocados, bananas, onions and potatoes all do well outside, so it's good practice to put them in designated baskets. Do note that keeping onions and potatoes in the same basket will make the potatoes sprout faster, and any fruits kept along with the banana will ripen too quickly for your liking.

The refrigerator also plays host to some of my favourite masalas. While we all agree that freshly-ground spice mixes give the best results, not many of us have the time to prepare them, so store-bought masalas are good enough for everyday cooking.

Doing a kitchen census periodically ensures that stuff close to expiry is used up quickly and ingredients past their expiry date are discarded. Of course, my kitchen census could be skewed slightly towards overstocking due to the recipe development and testing I had to do for this book, but here's the list of ingredients that I currently have in stock:

- **Beans:** Dried green peas, black-eyed peas (lobia), kidney beans (rajma), chickpeas (kabuli chana), green moong, whole Bengal gram (kala chana), moth beans (matki), horse gram (kulthi ka dal).

- **Grains:** Two to three varieties of rice, broken wheat (dalia), millets (bajra, ragi), barley (jau), oats (both instant and steel-cut).
- **Lentils/dal:** Husked, split pigeon peas (arhar/tur), moong, Egyptian lentils (masoor), Bengal gram (chana), black gram (urad).
- **Flours:** Corn meal (makki ka atta), millets (bajra), sorghum (jowar), rice flour, gram flour (besan), husked black gram flour (urad dal atta), buckwheat (kuttu).
- **Breakfast ingredients:** Beaten rice (poha), puffed rice (murmura), semolina (sooji), vermicelli (sevai), idli mix.
- **Spices (whole and ground):** Two to three varieties of dried red chillies, mustard, cumin (jeera), fenugreek (methi), pepper, cloves (laung), cinnamon (dalchini), cardamom (elaichi), fennel (saunf), coriander (dhania), asafoetida (hing), celery seeds, Bengali five-spice mix (panch phoran), nigella seeds (kalaunji), onion seeds, turmeric, dried mango powder (aamchoor), dried pomegranate seeds (anar dana), tamarind, etc.
- **Masala mixes:** Sambar powder, rasam powder, garam masala, subzi masala, pav bhaji masala, chole masala, pani puri masala, chat masala, pickle masala, pulao masala, sandwich masala, chai masala.
- **Sugar and salt:** Sugar, jaggery, iodized salt, rock salt.
- **Beverages:** Assorted tea leaves, coffee, cocoa.
- **Baking ingredients**: Baking soda, baking powder, chocolate, cocoa powder, cinnamon powder, etc.
- **Miscellaneous items:** Assorted packs of pasta and noodles.

The number of items you stock also depends on how many people you're looking to feed. Smaller families do better with stocking up on fewer ingredients. You could buy three to four varieties of beans this month and some other varieties the following month. Stocking up large quantities of too many ingredients can lead to wastage and spoilage.

Stocking Up for Healthy Cooking

Grains: Rice, broken wheat (dalia), millets – 2 varieties (bajra, ragi).

Lentils/dal: Pigeon peas, moong dal, husked Bengal gram, among others.

Beans: Green moong, moth beans, whole Bengal gram, kidney beans, chickpeas, etc.

Flours: Whole wheat flour (atta), rice flour, gram flour, millet flour, sorghum flour.

Fresh produce: Seasonal vegetables and fruits, herbs and greens.

Spices: Mustard, cumin, coriander, fenugreek, dried red chillies, fennel seeds, cloves, cinnamon and cardamom are some of the essential spices needed to stock up a fully-functional kitchen.

Oils, nuts and seeds: Cold-pressed oils, ghee, extra-virgin oils for salads. Almonds, walnuts, flaxseeds, sesame seeds, coconut, etc. to provide the much-needed healthy fats to your diet.

Dairy and soya products: Milk, yogurt, paneer, cheese, tofu.

Superfoods: Powdered or fresh Indian gooseberry (amla), flaxseeds, spirulina and moringa powder (both excellent for green smoothies), powdered or fresh turmeric. Other superfoods are already included in the categories of grains, spices, nuts, etc.

PERMIT

Menu Planning: How To Go about It and Why It Is Important

A menu plan is a bird's-eye view of meals to cook during the week. With some basic knowledge of nutrition, you can tell if there is a fair balance of macronutrients such as complex carbohydrates, proteins, veggies/fruits and healthy fats in your meals.

It also helps you while you shop and stock up. Impulsive and healthy don't partner well, after all. Your best shot at cooking healthy meals at home is to plan for them. Dal for lunch and a bean salad for dinner? No problem! You can simply cook them in the same pressure cooker in different compartments. If you've planned these meals in advance, you will be able to soak the beans the previous night.

The week I don't have a menu plan, you'll find me staring blankly into an open refrigerator waiting for a genie to rescue me. When I used to pack lunches for my kid, the weekly menu plan was my ultimate saviour. Even if you are a busy professional, carry your own packed lunch. With some planning, you can do it without much fuss in the mornings (or make the lunch meal at night and store it in an airtight container in the refrigerator). Plan out the three main meals of the day and stick to a list of healthy snacks such as air-popped corn, dark chocolate, roasted nuts (pre-portioned), hummus, seasonal fruits, etc.

As an added incentive, I will add here that planning out your meals makes economic sense. Buying just as much fresh produce as you need for the week ensures that nothing is left languishing at the bottom of the veggie crisper, waiting for its turn to end up in the compost pile. A menu plan also helps you use dry groceries systematically. Arrange the items you need for the week's menu in the front of your kitchen cabinets. If a spoonful each of three to four beans are left in their bottles, mix them together, soak overnight and make something like a sprouted moth bean curry (p. 176–177). Don't buy more groceries till all the bottles are empty. Kitchen management is no mean feat.

To get started with menu planning, you can use a worksheet on your computer or a menu planning template you can find on the Internet. The sheet should have fields for days of the week, the meals (breakfast, lunch, dinner, snacks), the preparation required and the shopping list. Populate the weekly menu chart with family favourites for some meals. Add some new healthy recipes that you have been meaning to try for some of the meals. Balance an elaborate dinner with a healthier breakfast and a light lunch such as a soup or a salad.

You'll find a few sample menus at the end of the book with recipes from the four sections. Fill in your own menu sheets, take a printout and stick it on your refrigerator every Sunday night. Not only will your family know what to expect for their next meal, I promise that it will also make you feel totally in control. A menu plan is also helpful if you have a cook. No more last-minute panicking over what to ask him/her to cook.

Basic Equipment: A Checklist

I completely understand the temptation to bring home every one of those shiny kitchen appliances you see in the store, but let's put on our practical hats here and look at a list of multipurpose workhorses that are truly worthy of occupying space in your kitchen. This list is also useful if you are setting up your kitchen afresh. Less is more and you will find it easier to cook in a non-cluttered space.

Gas stove (two to four burners): The gas stove you get depends on your family size and on how much you cook. A three-burner stove is good enough for most families, giving you enough wrist and elbow room to stir all three pans without burning yourself. The four-burner stove tends to get a bit cramped (although there are more spacious models available) if you plan to operate all four burners simultaneously. Some prefer to have at least one induction stove, which is portable and gives you a backup should you run out of LPG.

Oven and microwave: Welcome to the biggest dilemma faced by many of my readers. A convection oven or OTG allows you to bake cakes, breads, cookies, pizzas and other baked dishes. I would definitely recommend getting one if your family loves these dishes. If you have young kids at home, they are better off eating homemade cakes and bakes using real ingredients over the store-bought stuff. If you are setting up your kitchen from scratch, then planning for an in-built oven under the cooking hob saves counter space. You could then go for a small, rather basic, microwave oven which, if you ask me, is not an absolute must in the kitchen. Food can always be reheated on the stove top and that's all most people end up using the microwave for.

Mixer-grinder: This is the one thing an Indian kitchen cannot function without. The small mixer jar can also be used to grind spice powders, fresh masalas and whip up salad dressings. The larger jar can make smoothies, dips, dosa batters and chutneys. This is a long-term investment, so buy a good quality machine with a powerful motor (750 watts and above is great) and a proper warranty.

Food processor/chopper: This is optional, especially if you wield ninja-level knife skills, but it comes in handy when you need to chop a large quantity of veggies quickly. The drawback, though, is that it can only mince vegetable and not slice, julienne, grate, etc. A small food processor often comes with a hand blender attachment, which is useful to liquify dals and soups while still in the pan, so you don't have to worry about hot liquids splashing out of the blender.

Pressure cooker: Unless you want to spend most of your life by the cooking range, this buy for your kitchen is elementary, dear reader. Most cooks outside India (who are not Indians) do not use one, but I don't know of a single kitchen that would not benefit from this appliance. If you are a family of two, you can buy a larger one (7 litres) with compartments in which you can cook dal, rice and a vegetable at the same time, and a smaller one (2–3 litres) to prepare a curry, or for when you need to cook just one item. A pressure cooker makes quick work of thick-skinned beans such as chickpeas and kidney beans, and hard veggies like beetroots, turnips and potatoes. I also use the pressure cooker to make my 30-minute vegetable stock that works as a perfect base for soups.

Chopping boards and knives: Wooden boards look good and are sturdy, but they need maintenance. I once threw a wooden chopping board in the dishwasher because I wanted it squeaky clean and it came out in four parts. Plastic and glass chopping boards are also easy to clean and practical.

Coconut grater: This one occupies a VIP position in a South Indian kitchen. Leave it out if your food processor has a coconut grating attachment. I recommend the one that comes with a scraping blade at one end, a handle to rotate the blade at the other, and a vacuum seal at the bottom that keeps the equipment in place while you scrape the coconut.

Measuring and weighing equipment: These are essential for baked dishes and to follow recipes from cookbooks. All recipes in this book use a standard baking measuring cup. Serving spoons and cups vary vastly from kitchen to kitchen. It is difficult to convey a sense of proportion without using standard measures, so make sure you get one set of standard measuring cups and spoons. Digital kitchen weighing scales are useful for precise baking measurements of flour, butter, etc. If you follow diets where it is important to weigh out portions, these kitchen scales are a must.

Graters and peelers: A fine grater is a must for using ginger and garlic in recipes, as well as for making Indian-style salads and raitas. A good peeler not just peels but also gives you pretty ribbons of zucchini, carrots and radishes to make fun salads. You can also use them to make a fettuccini-like 'fake' pasta, if you're on a low carb diet. For this, check out my baked zucchini pasta recipe (p. 24–25).

Assorted equipment: A sauté pan (kadhai or wok) with a lid, two pans of different sizes with lids, a large pan for boiling pasta and noodles, a colander, a griddle (tava), board and rolling pin (chakla-belan) to roll out rotis, tongs, a flat steel spatula, a silicon spatula to stir sauces, etc., a rounded ladle for dal, three mixing bowls in different sizes (for salads, batters, baking mixes).

Helpful Healthy Cooking Tips

- When cooking ingredients with a long cooking time (for example, brown or red rice, beetroots, chickpeas, rajma, whole wheat pasta, etc.) cook a bigger batch so that you already have one healthy ingredient (or two) sitting in the refrigerator when you plan your next meal.
- When in doubt, soak some beans overnight. These can be used in salads for lunch or to cook a khichdi or misal for dinner. Don't want to use the soaked beans immediately? Sprout them. Drain and put them in a bottle to sprout. Make use of the sprouts in a salad, pulao, khichdi, smoothies or along with vegetables in a curry.
- Prepare a triple batch of dry ingredients for pancakes and store it in bottles or sealable plastic bags. This way you only have to measure once for three breakfasts.
- Prepare a dry mix for instant dosas by combining wheat flour, oat flour, corn meal, sorghum flour or any other combination you like with a dash of spices such as black pepper, dried curry leaves, etc. and you are minutes away from a hearty dosa.
- Use the pressure cooker to its full capacity using separators. For this, it is useful to have a general idea of foods that have similar cooking times. For example, beetroot and brown rice both take around 15 minutes on low heat, potato and lentils cook for similar times.
- When grinding a fresh paste for a curry or a sambar, double the quantity, freeze half and make sure you jot this down in your weekly menu for another day.
- The same rule applies for salad dressings. Prepare a full bottle and, as long as there is no fresh garlic or herbs swimming in your dressing, it will do just fine. You can always add the fresh ingredient to the required quantity of dressing just before use.
- Salads in glass jars are very popular. Chop and prep once for five salads during the week. Carrots, sprouts, cooked beans, hardier leaves like kale, cooked beetroots, radish slices, etc. will stay fresh for a few days. Make sure the bottles are airtight and store in the refrigerator.
- While cleaning and prepping fresh produce, make sure you wash veggies, fruits and green leaves well. As this is a given, it is not included in the steps for the recipes. Soaking produce in a small tub of water with a mix of lemon juice and vinegar (1 tbsp each) helps remove most of the pesticide residue.

- For cooking, I recommend cold-pressed groundnut, coconut, mustard, sesame or olive oil as per a recipe's requirement. Reserve extra-virgin olive oil for salads. Use regular olive oils in recipes that involve heating the oil.
- Millets like foxtail, little millet, kodo, etc., don't need any soaking. Wash, drain and combine with two parts water (2 cups water for 1 cup millet) and pressure cook for 5 minutes over low heat after the cooker reaches full pressure (first whistle). If using the stovetop boiling method, it takes roughly 12 minutes to cook.
- Barley, brown rice and bamboo rice need to be soaked for 4–5 hours before cooking. It is most efficient to pressure cook such grains. Drain the soaked grains and combine them with 2½–3 times the water. After two whistles, cook over low heat for 15–20 minutes.
- Most whole beans like green moong, moth beans, horse gram, fenugreek seeds, etc., can be sprouted and used in salads or cooked dishes. Wash the beans or seeds and soak them overnight in plenty of water. The following morning, drain and rinse them thoroughly. Either tie the beans in a muslin cloth and put them in a covered bowl on the kitchen counter or place in a large glass jar with the lid loosely closed. In hot weather, it is easy to get around half-inch long sprouts in just one day. In cooler weather, rinse the sprouts after 24 hours and return to the muslin cloth or bottle. In 48 hours, the beans will be well sprouted. Sprouting increases the volume of the beans considerably. Check if a recipe asks for a half-cup of dried or sprouted beans. For example, a half-cup of dried moth beans (about 100 grams) will yield a little over two cups of sprouts.
- Getting a perfectly ripe avocado is every avocado lover's dream, but it is also an incredibly hard thing to find in a local market. However, I have gotten the better of these pesky avocados with a life-saving tip: Wrap each avocado in newspaper and keep it in a fruit basket with bananas, apples or papaya. The other ripening fruit lets out ethylene dioxide gas that helps in ripening the avocados. Press through the wrapping paper every day to check on them. When you feel the flesh yielding to pressure, use immediately or refrigerate them.

How to Make Amazing Salads at Home

I've been conducting salad-making workshops for a few years now and the response has been very heartening. This short section is to help you make salads a part of your diet without being intimidated by them. Remember: If you can make a chaat, you can make a salad!

My recipes will show you that you can make beautiful salads using fairly common ingredients and techniques. A cold-pressed oil (for best health benefits) and a bottle of vinegar of your choice can go a long way in pepping up your salads. Here, I'm sharing with you almost all the tips that I teach in my workshops:

Greens: For best results, make your salad when the ingredients are fresh. Wash and dry the salad greens just before putting together the salad so that they don't wilt.
Fill the kitchen sink or a large bowl with water. Select fresh green leaves and immerse them in the water. Allow to sit for 5–10 minutes. Any soil or grit will settle down at the bottom of the bowl or sink. Fish the leaves out and transfer them to another bowl. Now drain the water from the first bowl, refill it with clean water and repeat this process once more. Remove the leaves, shake off the excess water, wrap them in clean, absorbent kitchen towels or use a salad spinner to dry out all the moisture. Wet leaves make poor salads.

If you don't have access to fresh salad greens, you can still make a salad using local greens like fenugreek leaves and amaranth (chauli). Take care to choose the smaller and more tender leaves. You can also make a wide assortment of salads that involve no leafy greens.

Chopping techniques: Try different cuts of the same vegetable to make a variety of salads. Take carrot for example: You can cut it into thick chunks and roast it in the oven for a roasted veggie salad. You can use a julienne peeler and turn the carrot into noodles to use in an Asian rice-noodle salad. You can also grate the carrot, combine it with toasted peanuts and a tempering of mustard seeds, chillies and curry leaves to make an Indian-style salad. Finally, you can finely slice the carrot and combine it with finely sliced cucumbers, onions, tomatoes and radishes to make an Indian-restaurant style 'green salad'.

Flavour-boosters: These aromatic ingredients can be used in small quantities to add oomph to a salad. Think ginger, citrus zest, roasted garlic, smoked paprika, rosemary,

sesame oil, mustard oil and so on! A little goes a long way, so use these carefully. These flavour-boosters are most often added as a part of the salad dressing, so that the flavour is uniformly distributed throughout the salad, ensuring a zesty bite in every forkful.

The crunch element: This adds the fun element to a salad, often taking it from dull and boring to something you want to eat. Be it toasted nuts, oven-baked croutons or baked crackers, the crunch factor must not be ignored. Add this to the bowl just before serving.

The dressing: The most impressive salad dressings – that have people licking the bowl clean – have that critical balance of sweet, spicy, tangy and salty flavours. If you think about it, it is quite like the assortment of chutneys atop streetside chaat which gives it that addictive quality. Use good quality extra-virgin olive oil or cold-pressed coconut oil to infuse some healthy fats into your salad via the dressing.

Tossing: Use the largest bowl you have to toss salads. This prevents the ingredients from getting bruised and thereby losing their freshness before they reach the serving bowl. Use your fingertips or wooden salad servers. These inflict the least pressure on the delicate ingredients.

Garnishes: Special garnishes such as caramelized nuts, cheese, croutons, etc. are best served on top of individual portions of salad. There are two practical reasons for this. One, everyone gets a fair share of the special ingredient, and two, this prevents ingredients like cheese from being squished to a mush during the tossing and the crisp ingredients from turning soggy.

Serving: Some salads do well with a bit of rest in the refrigerator, and some need to be served immediately after tossing. Hearty grain salads like the herby bamboo rice salad (p. 113–114) absorb flavours better after being chilled for 2–3 hours. Leaf-heavy salads do better on being served immediately as they tend to start wilting and losing water once tossed with the dressing.

Some Recipe Guidelines

- All measurements (cups, spoons) are based on standard baking cup measurements:

  1 teaspoon (tsp) = 5 ml
  1 tablespoon (tbsp) = 15 ml (3 tsp)
  1 cup = 240 ml

- Please read the recipe fully before starting.
- Ingredients appear in the order in which they are used in the recipe.
- If you see the word 'divided' next to an ingredient, it means the ingredient is used more than once in the recipe. This will be specified in the steps.
- Always preheat the oven to the required temperature before starting to bake.
- All recipes in this book have slightly less than normal levels of salt. Feel free to adjust as per your taste.
- All fruits and vegetables must be washed, cleaned and wiped dry before you start on the recipe.
- Soak herbs and garnishes in a bowl of cold water when you start cooking the dish. They will be springy and fresh when it's time to use them.
- Keep all spices and tempering (tadka) ingredients on hand before you heat the oil.
- Don't use extra-virgin olive oil for cooking purposes. Use regular olive oil or any other cold-pressed oil.

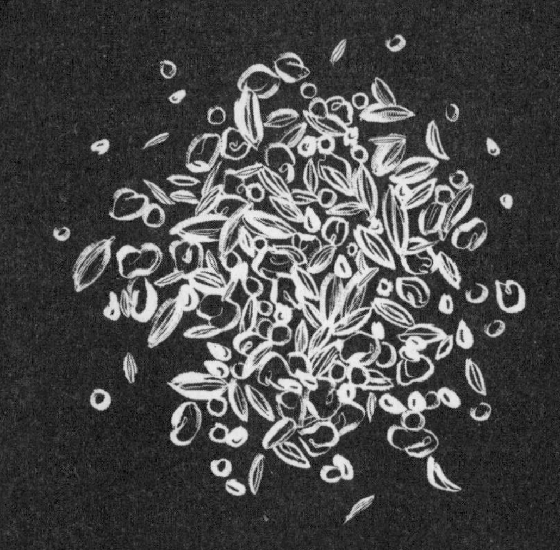

eat the rainbow

We in India are blessed with an incredible range of produce in terms of fruits and vegetables, which we often take for granted. A walk around the local vegetable and fruit market in any city makes me giddy with happiness. I remember making a trip to the local *rythu bazaar* in Hyderabad with my neighbour and coming home with 20 kilos of tomatoes that were being sold at ₹3 per kilo. And all this for a family of two adults! Nothing fuels my love for cooking more than fresh produce. Salads, curries, sauces, chutneys, snacks – the list of things you can make from fresh fruits and vegetables is endless.

Eating at least five servings of fruit and vegetables a day helps you stock up on all the vitamins and minerals that you need for good health, reducing the risk of chronic diseases. Fruits and vegetables come loaded with fibre, an all-important nutrient for a healthy gut, preventing diabetes and even heart disease. Produce of each colour comes with its own range of phytochemicals that are full of disease-preventing, immunity-boosting, anti-inflammatory antioxidants. But the best part is the colour, flavour and texture they add to every dish!

Five-a-day is a popular concept in many countries, pushing people to get at least 5 x 80 gram portions of fruits and vegetables a day. If you are already at five-a-day, then you can always aim higher. While fresh is best, all other versions of produce, such as frozen, canned, cooked, fermented and 100 per cent juices are also considered in these servings. As per the MyPlate nutrition guidelines, half the plate should be reserved for fruits and vegetables.

So the next time you serve yourself a meal, keep an eye out for the colours on your plate – the more the better!

The Happy Salad

I could just say, 'Open your refrigerator, pull out all the yellow fruits and veggies you find and make a salad', but this is a cookbook so I'll be a little more elaborate. Yellow is a colour that never fails to cheer me up as it is a colour I associate with sunshine and happiness. The name 'Beta-Carotene Salad' would be apt but 'The Happy Salad' sounds so much better!

SERVES 2–4

THE SALAD

1 yellow bell pepper
½ cup fresh sweetcorn kernels (or a sweetcorn cob)
1 cup yellow pumpkin cubes (heaped)
1 ripe mango (if in season)
2 tsp olive oil

THE DRESSING

4–5 stalks thyme, fresh
1 tbsp extra-virgin olive oil
3 tbsp fresh orange juice
1 tbsp honey
¼ tsp smoked paprika
¼ tsp salt

1 Remove the pith and seeds of the bell pepper and discard. Dice the flesh into small pieces.

2 Shuck a fresh sweetcorn cob to get roughly ½ a cup of kernels.

3 Ensure the pumpkin is diced into fairly small pieces so that all the veggies cook at the same time. Dice the mango into similar-sized cubes as the pumpkin.

4 Heat the olive oil in a cast-iron pan or a heavy frying pan over moderate to high heat.

5 Add the vegetables and corn kernels to the pan. Let the veggies get a few golden-brown spots on the surface.

6 Lower the heat, cover the pan with a lid and cook for 5–7 minutes till the pumpkin cubes are cooked through but retain their shape.

THE DRESSING

1 Strip the thyme leaves off the stalks and crush them with your fingertips before adding them to a small bowl.

2 Add the remaining ingredients for the dressing and whisk well with a fork till you get a thick dressing. (You can also pulse the ingredients in the small jar of the food processor to prepare the dressing.)

TO SERVE

1. Transfer the cooked veggies and mango on to a platter.

2. Pour the dressing over the salad and serve.

You can use other similarly-coloured fruits and vegetables to make a monochrome salad like this one in green or red.

Yellow fruits and vegetables are abundant in beta-carotene, which is the precursor of vitamin A in the human body. The phenolic antioxidants in corn can help reduce the complications of raised blood-sugar levels in diabetic patients.

CALORIES (KCAL)	PROTEIN	FATS	CARBOHYDRATES	FIBRE
157.9	1.7	6.4	24.4	2.4

(per serving)

The Ultimate Superfood Burger

In 2016, a London nutritionist created a burger with more than 50 superfood ingredients including everything from cacao to bee pollen and seaweed to fermented soya beans. This is my take on a superfood burger – deep pink in colour, and packed with texture and flavour.

MAKES 4 burgers

THE PATTIES

- 2 small beetroots
- 1 cup moong sprouts (heaped)
- 3 tbsp almond meal or gram flour (besan)
- 1 tbsp flaxseed meal
- 2–3 tbsp finely chopped green garlic
- 1 tsp coconut oil
- 3 cloves garlic, finely minced
- 1 medium-sized onion, finely sliced
- 12 spinach leaves
- ¼ tsp turmeric powder
- ½ tsp cumin powder (jeera)
- ¾ tsp salt
- ½ tsp black pepper, freshly ground

TO COOK THE PATTIES

THE PATTIES

1 Wash the beetroots well and put them into a pressure cooker with just enough water to cover them. Close the pressure cooker with the lid and the pressure weight plugged in.

2 After the cooker reaches full pressure (first whistle), lower the flame and cook for another 12–15 minutes. Open the cooker after the pressure subsides.

3 Peel the beetroots and grate them into a bowl. Put the grated beetroot in a sieve placed over a bowl, squeezing out all the liquid.

4 Blanch the moong sprouts by boiling them in 1 cup of water for 2–3 minutes. Drain well and grind to a coarse paste.

5 Mix the grated beetroots, moong sprouts paste, almond meal or gram flour, flaxseed meal and green garlic in a large bowl.

6 Heat the coconut oil in a saute pan. Sauté the garlic and onion for 3–4 minutes.

7 Add the spinach leaves and turmeric powder. Sauté till the spinach wilts.

8 Remove from heat and mix with the other ingredients in the bowl.

9 Season the mixture with cumin powder, salt and pepper. Knead well to get a smooth dough-like mixture.

10 Divide the mix into 4 portions and shape into patties. Arrange them on a flat dish. Cover with cling wrap and refrigerate for at least 2 hours.

2 tbsp olive oil (approx.)

THE BURGERS

4 whole-wheat buns

Non-dairy cashew cheesy spread (p. 189) or regular cheese spread

Lettuce leaves

Avocado slices or tomato slices

Any hot sauce of choice

TO COOK THE PATTIES

1 Place a flat pan over moderate heat. When hot, smear it with ½ tbsp olive oil and place the patties on the pan.

2 Allow to cook on each side for 10–12 minutes, till lightly golden on the outside. (Handle the burgers gently.)

3 Drizzle 1–1½ tsp of olive oil around each burger to allow it to crisp up.

THE BURGERS

1 Slice the buns midway.

2 Smear some cashew cheese or regular cheese spread on each half.

3 On one half of each burger bun, place a lettuce leaf, a burger patty and avocado or tomato slices.

4 Cover with the other half and serve immediately with any hot sauce of your choice on the side.

See photograph 19 of colour insert.

You can substitute sweet potatoes and mashed, cooked chickpeas (kabuli chana) for beetroots and moong sprouts respectively.

Do not discard the leftover beetroot juice and the water used to boil the moong sprouts. You can add a pinch of pepper and drink it.

Beetroot juice increases nitric oxide levels in our body, thereby improving blood flow, respiratory functions and athletic performance.

CALORIES (KCAL)	PROTEIN	FATS	CARBOHYDRATES	FIBRE
345.8	9.3	18.6	35.7	8.6

(per serving)

Broccoli and Green Peas with Bengali Five-Spice Mix

The Bengali five-spice mix (panch phoran) is a mix of five whole spices – nigella seeds, aniseed, fenugreek seeds, black mustard seeds and cumin seeds – in equal proportions. It is used in Bengali and Odia cuisines, adding tiny but intense bursts of flavour and crunch. The use of mustard oil and panch phoran in this recipe is inspired from one of my favourite Indian cuisines.

SERVES 2–4

- 1 medium-sized broccoli, broken into florets
- 2 tbsp cold-pressed mustard oil
- 1½ tsp Bengali five-spice mix (panch phoran)
- 2 green chillies, finely chopped
- 4 cloves garlic, finely minced
- 1 cup fresh green peas
- ½ tsp salt

1 Wash the broccoli florets in plenty of water. Drain and keep aside.

2 Heat the mustard oil in a deep, wide pan.

3 Once it is smoking hot add the panch phoran, green chillies and garlic. Stir over moderate heat for 30 seconds.

4 Add the broccoli florets and green peas, and mix well with the seasoned oil.

5 Pour ¼ cup of water over the vegetables. Cover and steam cook for 7–8 minutes, till the green peas are tender and the broccoli is cooked but retains a bite.

6 Serve hot with dal and rice or as a vegetable side dish with any meal.

You can make your own panch phoran by mixing nigella seeds, aniseed, fenugreek seeds, black mustard seeds and cumin seeds in equal parts.

You can also use frozen green peas if fresh green peas are out of season.

1 cup of broccoli gives you over 2 grams of both protein and fibre. A minimal glycaemic load makes it an excellent vegetable for diabetics. Half a cup of green peas provides 4 grams of both fibre and protein. You can also try these two vegetables in other dishes such as salads and soups or with pasta.

GARDENING TIP:

For a fun gardening experiment, sow the panch phoran spices in a shallow tray of soil. Spray water over the soil everyday and in 10 days, you can harvest a mix of micro greens.

CALORIES (KCAL)	PROTEIN	FATS	CARBOHYDRATES	FIBRE
116.9	3.8	7.6	9.2	4.3

(per serving)

Potato Lettuce Salad with Chilli Garlic Dressing

This is your humble potato salad turned completely on its head: Hearty potatoes on a substratum of fresh lettuce and drenched with a garlicky tadka (tempering). Best to make more of this rather than less, because everyone is going to go after the bowl.

SERVES 2–4

4 medium-sized potatoes, boiled and peeled

THE TEMPERING

¼ tsp carom seeds (ajwain)
¾ tsp cumin seeds (jeera)
4–5 black peppercorns
3 tbsp groundnut oil
10–12 cloves garlic, finely chopped
3 green chillies, finely chopped
2 dried red chillies, broken into bits
A pinch of asafoetida (hing) powder
¼ tsp turmeric powder

THE DRESSING

1 lemon, juiced
1 tsp salt
1 tsp grated jaggery

Cut the boiled potatoes into chunks.

THE SEASONING

1 Lightly toast the carom seeds, cumin seeds and black peppercorns in a heavy-bottomed pan. Remove from the pan and cool.

2 Crush lightly and keep aside.

3 Heat the groundnut oil in the same pan. Once the oil is hot, lower the heat and add the green and red chillies, garlic, asafoetida powder, turmeric powder and the crushed spice mix.

4 Allow this to steep in the oil over the lowest heat setting for 8–10 minutes. If you feel that the oil is still very hot, turn off the heat. (The difference between this process and a tadka is that you are allowing the spices to release their flavours into the oil at a much lower temperature over a longer time, while a tadka takes mere seconds.)

THE DRESSING

1 Remove the pan with the seasoning mix from the heat. Add the lemon juice, salt and jaggery, stirring to combine well.

TO SERVE

1 Combine the potato chunks and onions with half of the prepared dressing and half of the lettuce leaves in a large bowl.

TO SERVE

1 medium-sized onion, finely sliced

3 cups roughly chopped lettuce leaves

2 Layer the remaining lettuce leaves on a platter. Top with the tossed potato-lettuce mix. Drizzle the remaining dressing over the top.

3 Serve warm or chilled.

You can prepare a larger quantity of this dressing and infuse the oil with spices of your liking. Store the cooled oil in an airtight bottle and you can refrigerate it for a week or so. It makes an excellent dressing for a rice bowl or any other salad that needs to be perked up.

Refrigerating cooked potatoes makes the starch in them retrograde resistant, preventing a spike in blood sugar or insulin. It resists digestion in the stomach, reaches the colon intact, behaving like a prebiotic for the good bacteria, thereby improving gut health and does not cause a spike in blood-sugar or insulin levels.

CALORIES (KCAL)	PROTEIN	FATS	CARBOHYDRATES	FIBRE
184.0	2.5	10.5	20.7	2.3

(per serving)

Roasted Pineapple Chilli Chutney

This chutney will be completely at home on an Indian thali. You can also serve it with nachos or crackers. The process of roasting the pineapple and chillies adds a solid dose of flavour to the chutney.

MAKES ¾ cup

- 8 Bhavnagri green chillies (*bajji* chillies)
- 400 g fresh pineapple cubes
- 2 tsp groundnut oil
- ½ tsp rock salt
- 1 tsp yellow mustard seeds

Preheat the oven to 200°C. Line a baking tray with parchment paper or aluminium foil and keep it handy.

1 Pinch off the stems of the green chillies. Slit lengthwise and scrape out the membranes and seeds with a teaspoon.

2 Toss the pineapple chunks and prepared chillies in oil. Arrange in a single layer on the prepared baking tray.

3 Place the tray in the topmost groove of the preheated oven and roast for 25 minutes at 200°C, or till the chillies and pineapple chunks have brown spots on them.

4 Once slightly cooled, transfer to a food processor and grind to a coarse paste along with the mustard seeds.

5 Store the chutney in an airtight glass jar. Refrigerate and use within 2–3 days.

Mustard seeds add a zing to this chutney. If you can't find yellow mustard seeds, substitute them with black mustard seeds. If you don't prefer the taste of mustard, leave them out. The chutney tastes pretty amazing even without it. You can smear the pineapple chutney on two slices of bread, add your favourite cheese, and grill in a sandwich toaster for a sassy sandwich.

Pineapple contains an enzyme called bromelain that aids in the digestion of proteins. It is also an anti-inflammatory enzyme that helps with joint pains and minor muscle injuries. Make sure you go for fresh pineapples and not the canned ones soaked in syrup.

CALORIES (KCAL)	PROTEIN	FATS	CARBOHYDRATES	FIBRE
101.7	1.1	3.4	17.4	4.1

Roasted Carrot Soup with Basil Oil

Roasting a root vegetable always gives it a flavour upgrade. The spicy notes of basil and the sweetness of the roasted carrots are a match made in culinary heaven. Serve with a hunk of crusty sourdough bread to make a complete meal.

SERVES 2

THE SOUP

- 3 large carrots, cut into small pieces
- 4 large cloves garlic, unpeeled
- 2 tsp olive oil
- ½ tsp salt
- 400 ml water
- Black pepper, freshly ground, to taste

THE BASIL OIL

- 14–16 fresh Italian basil leaves, chopped
- 2 tbsp extra-virgin olive oil
- ½ a lemon, juiced

THE GARNISH

- A small handful of micro greens (see cooking notes) or fresh sprouts
- 2 tbsp toasted seeds (a mix of sunflower, white sesame, pumpkin and flax)

THE SOUP

1 Preheat the oven to 180°C.

2 Toss the carrots and garlic in 2 tsp of olive oil and arrange them in a single layer on a baking tray.

3 Place the tray in the centre of the preheated oven and roast for 40 minutes. It is cooked well when the carrots yield to thumb pressure.

4 Transfer the contents of the baking tray to a blender. Blend along with the water to a fine puree.

5 Pour the puree into a medium-sized pan. Season with salt and pepper and bring to a simmer over moderate heat. Turn off the heat.

THE BASIL OIL

1 Put the chopped basil leaves, extra-virgin olive oil and lemon juice in the small jar of a food processor.

2 Pulse 3–4 times till the basil is infused into the oil.

TO SERVE

1 Divide the soup into two large soup bowls.

2 Garnish with a drizzle of the herby oil, a sprinkle of micro greens and the toasted seeds.

See photograph 20 of colour insert.

You can roast 1 green apple, chopped into chunks, along with the carrots to add a touch of tartness to the soup. You can also prepare extra portions, which you can freeze and thaw later in the week for a quick dinner.

Micro greens contain over 40 times the nutrients found in mature leaves. For example, coriander micro greens have abundant beta carotene and lutein, both excellent for eye health. Carrots are loaded with fibre which keeps you feeling full for a long time.

GARDENING TIP:

Micro greens are the first tiny green shoots that appear in a germinating seed. Grow your own by sowing seeds or sprouts in shallow trays. Use as a garnish on soups and salads. Carrots can be grown in pots that are at least 1 foot deep. Make sure the soil is light, compost rich and free of any stones. It takes around 2–2½ months to harvest carrots. Green leafy tops can be used in pesto, stews and soups.

CALORIES (KCAL)	PROTEIN	FATS	CARBOHYDRATES	FIBRE
246.8	2.5	20.7	13.7	3.9

(per serving)

Roasted Fruit Salad with Honey Cream and Mint

This is a one-of-a-kind fruit salad. Roasting fruits is commonplace in crumbles but that involves the addition of not-so-healthy ingredients such as refined flour and sugar. This almost-dessert harnesses the natural sweetness of fruits, and the dried mint and fennel seeds give it a lingering flavour.

SERVES 2

THE SALAD

1 medium-sized apple
1 medium-sized pear
2 cups pineapple cubes
1 cup seedless black grapes
½ tsp + 1½ tsp olive oil
¼ tsp salt

THE HONEY CREAM

100 ml coconut cream or whipping cream
1 tbsp honey

THE GARNISH

1 tsp fennel (saunf) seeds
1 tsp dried mint powder

THE SALAD

1 Preheat the oven to 200°C. Line a baking tray with parchment paper or aluminium foil.

2 Cut the apple and pear in half. Core and cut into bite-sized pieces, keeping them similar in size to the pineapple cubes. (You don't have to peel the apple and pear.)

3 Put the apple, pear and pineapple in a bowl. Keep aside.

4 Slice the grapes in half, toss in ½ tsp of olive oil and keep aside.

5 Toss the pineapple, apple and pear in 1½ tsp of olive oil and arrange them in a single layer on the prepared baking tray.

6 Place the tray in the centre of the preheated oven and roast for 15 minutes.

7 Pull the tray out and add the grapes to the partly roasted fruits.

8 Reduce the temperature to 180°C and return the tray to the oven for 10 minutes.

9 Transfer the roasted fruits on to a serving platter and allow to cool to room temperature.

10 Place in the refrigerator to chill.

THE HONEY CREAM

1 Add the coconut cream to a chilled bowl. Whisk using an electric whisk, till it is fluffy. (If using packaged coconut cream, use only the thicker part, reserving the watery milk for another recipe or a smoothie.)

2 If using whipping cream, whisk into soft peaks.

3 Towards the end of the whisking process, add the honey and mix gently.

4 Pour into a small serving bowl and refrigerate for 30 minutes.

THE GARNISH

1 Lightly toast the fennel seeds in a small pan and remove from heat.

2 Once cool, crush to a coarse powder using a mortar and pestle.

3 Mix with the mint powder.

TO SERVE

1 Spoon some of the coconut cream or whipped cream over the roasted fruits. Sprinkle the fennel-mint powder on top.

2 Serve chilled.

I usually buy ready-to-cook/eat pineapple cubes or slices from the fruit counter of the supermarket. If you don't have access to cut pineapple, then go for canned fruit, preferably not soaked in sugar syrup. Pat any excess moisture off and proceed with the recipe.

This dessert is perfect for those who don't consume refined sugar. Unlike baking with fruits, this recipe does not call for any butter, flour and sugar.

GARDENING TIP:
Mint is one of the easiest herbs to grow in pots. Get saplings from the nursery and repot in compost enriched soil. Make sure the pots get enough sun. Excess mint can be oven dried and stored as a powder.

CALORIES (KCAL)	PROTEIN	FATS	CARBOHYDRATES	FIBRE
291.2	2.0	15.4	37.4	8.1

(per serving)

Medley of Gourds in Coconut Milk

If you have no special liking for everyday Indian vegetables like bottle gourd, ridge gourd and pumpkin, this curry-in-a-hurry will make you change your mind. Get started on this curry while the rice is cooking and you'll be enjoying a comforting meal in less than 20 minutes.

SERVES 2

THE VEGETABLES

½ small bottle gourd (lauki)
150 g dark-yellow pumpkin
½ a small ridge gourd (toori)
½ tsp turmeric powder
½ tsp salt
1 tbsp coconut oil
150 ml coconut milk

THE SPICE PASTE

½" fresh ginger, peeled
3 cloves garlic
1 small onion, quartered
2 fresh red chillies

THE GARNISH

Black pepper, freshly ground, to taste

THE VEGETABLES

1 Choose tender gourds for this stew. Peel and dice the bottle gourd and pumpkin into large chunks. Peel and slice the ridge gourd in ½-inch thick slices.

2 Add ¼ cup of water, salt and turmeric powder to a pan and bring to boil over moderate heat.

3 Add the vegetable chunks. Cover and allow them to cook on a slow simmer. This should take 7–8 minutes. You can also pressure-cook the vegetables. Take the pressure cooker off the heat as soon as it reaches full pressure (first whistle). The boiling method ensures that the veggies don't turn into a mush.

THE SPICE PASTE

1 Grind all the ingredients for the spice paste into a smooth paste.

2 Heat the coconut oil in a medium-sized sauté pan. Add the paste and sauté over low to moderate heat for 5–6 minutes.

TO FINISH

1 Pour in the coconut milk. (Freshly-extracted coconut milk has the best flavour, but using packaged coconut milk is totally fine.) Bring this to a simmer.

2 Drain the cooked gourds, reserving the liquid (if any).

3 Add the vegetables to the simmering coconut milk.

4 Thin down with the reserved liquid if needed. (You can season and then drink this reserved liquid as a clear soup too.)

5 Check for seasoning.

TO SERVE

1 Transfer to a serving bowl, garnish with some freshly-ground black pepper. Serve hot.

In winter you can prepare this stew using seasonal vegetables such as carrots, green peas and cauliflower. Using just bottle gourd and ridge gourd makes it a low-carb curry. Zucchini is a good substitute for either of the gourds.

Combining this stew with brown rice or quinoa makes it a gluten-free, vegan meal. To up the protein content of the dish, add some cooked beans or diced tofu to the curry.

CALORIES (KCAL)	PROTEIN	FATS	CARBOHYDRATES	FIBRE
282.5	3.7	24.8	14.3	5.4

(per serving)

Purple Cabbage with Leafy Greens (Thoran)

Thoran is a simple South-Indian vegetable preparation made with carrots, beans, cabbage or a mix of two or more vegetables. Using a mix of purple cabbage and green leafy vegetables makes it a more vibrant dish.

SERVES 4

THE TEMPERING
- 2 tbsp coconut oil
- 1 tsp cumin seeds (jeera)
- 2 sprigs fresh curry leaves
- 3–4 green chillies, slit
- 4 cloves garlic, coarsely crushed

THE VEGETABLES
- 6 cups finely shredded purple cabbage
- 3 cups finely shredded greens such as radish leaves
- ¾ tsp salt

THE GARNISH
- 2 tbsp grated fresh coconut
- Fresh curry leaves

THE TEMPERING

1 Heat the coconut oil in a large frying pan over moderate heat.

2 Add the cumin seeds. When the seeds pop, add the curry leaves, green chillies and garlic.

3 Stir over moderate heat for 10 seconds.

THE VEGETABLES

1 Add the shredded cabbage, greens and salt to the tempering. Toss well over high heat for 1–2 minutes.

2 Reduce the heat, cover and steam cook for 7–8 minutes. Take care to stir through once every 3–4 minutes, sprinkling some water if you feel that the cabbage is sticking to the bottom of the pan.

3 Remove from heat. The cabbage and greens should be just-cooked, while retaining their colour and a slight crunch.

TO SERVE

1 Put in a serving bowl and garnish with grated coconut and curry leaves.

See photograph 17 of colour insert.

You can prepare thoran *using any fresh green leafy vegetable such as spinach or amaranth. As it is a minimalistic dish using fresh produce yields the best results.*

CALORIES (KCAL)	PROTEIN	FATS	CARBOHYDRATES	FIBRE
166.4	3.6	11.8	13.3	4.7

(per serving)

Rainbow Salad with Citrus and Olive Oil Dressing

These dishes don't necessarily sport the VIBGYOR pattern: An array of striking colours in any dish qualifies it for the 'rainbow' tag. My version of the rainbow salad promises to brighten up your table.

SERVES 2–4

THE SALAD
- 1 large red bell pepper
- 1 large yellow bell pepper
- 1 large green bell pepper
- 1 large orange carrot
- 2 cups shredded purple cabbage
- 1 tbsp olive oil

THE DRESSING
- ¼ cup extra-virgin olive oil
- 2 tbsp apple cider vinegar
- ¼ cup freshly-squeezed orange juice
- 1 orange, zested
- ½ tsp salt
- 1 tbsp honey

THE SALAD

1 Preheat the oven to 180°C. Line a large baking tray with parchment paper or aluminium foil and keep it handy.

2 Remove and discard the seeds and pith from the bell peppers. Scrub the carrots. Cut the vegetables into thin strips.

3 In a large bowl, toss the chopped vegetables in olive oil. Arrange them in a single layer on the prepared baking tray. Put the tray in the centre of the preheated oven and roast for 20 minutes at 180°C.

THE DRESSING

1 Blend all the ingredients for the dressing in the small jar of a mixer until thick and creamy.

TO SERVE

1 Return the oven-roasted veggies to a large bowl and toss in the prepared dressing. Serve warm or chilled.

See photograph 25 of colour insert.

For roasting, you can choose other vegetables such as sweet potatoes, green and yellow zucchini, and aubergine (baingan). The more colours you manage to pack in, the merrier.

You can also place a hearty portion of this salad over lettuce or roti/tortilla to make a healthy wrap.

You can use purple cabbage to bulk up any dish without adding too many calories. A cup of raw, chopped purple cabbage provides only 27 calories and almost 2 grams of fibre. It will also keep you feeling full for longer.

CALORIES (KCAL)	PROTEIN	FATS	CARBOHYDRATES	FIBRE
206.9	1.9	16.1	16.1	3.9

(per serving)

Roasted Aubergine and Labneh on Pita

In 2016 I was fortunate enough to be a part of a bloggers' trip to Jordan. It was there that I came across Labneh, a very popular Middle Eastern dish, that can be served as part of a breakfast, lunch or dinner spread. Topped with a pool of extra-virgin olive oil or a sprinkling of *za'atar* or sumac (found in speciality stores), this is quite a delicacy. Labneh takes 4–5 hours of inactive cooking time, so do prepare for it in advance. This dish makes for a pretty appetizer or can be one of the courses of a Mediterranean meal.

SERVES 2–4

THE LABNEH
400 g yogurt
A pinch of salt
A pinch of red paprika
1 tbsp extra-virgin olive oil

THE AUBERGINE
1 large aubergine (baingan)
Salt to sprinkle + extra salt
2 tbsp olive oil

TO ASSEMBLE
Mini pitas
Za'atar

THE GARNISH
Fresh pomegranate arils
Fresh mint leaves

THE LABNEH

1 Line a fine-meshed sieve with 2 layers of muslin cloth and place it over a bowl.

2 Tip the yogurt over the lined sieve and place the entire set-up in the refrigerator for 4–6 hours, till the yogurt resembles a ball of soft cheese. Transfer the hung yogurt to a bowl.

3 Whip the yogurt lightly with a fork to break down any clumps and to get a smooth texture. Mix in the salt and paprika. Smoothen out the top and drizzle extra-virgin olive oil over it.

4 Keep refrigerated.

THE AUBERGINE

1 Preheat the oven to 190°C.

2 Slice the aubergine into ¼-inch thick slices.

3 Rub salt over the slices and leave in a sieve for 15 minutes to drain out excess liquid.

4 Pat dry the aubergine slices. Transfer to a bowl and add the olive oil.

5 Arrange the slices in a single layer on a large baking tray.

6 Place the tray in the centre of the oven and roast for 10–12 minutes till cooked through and soft.

7 Sprinkle a pinch of salt over the roasted aubergine slices.

TO ASSEMBLE

1 Slice the mini pitas horizontally through the centre to get two slices. Toast the slices lightly if preferred.

2 Smear a teaspoon of labneh over each slice.

3 Top with 1–2 slices of roasted aubergine.

4 Season with a sprinkling of *za'atar.*

TO SERVE

1 Garnish with pomegranate arils and mint leaves and serve.

See photograph 27 of colour insert.

You can also use roasted zucchini or bell peppers as a topping for the pitas. Labneh can also be served as part of a mezze platter along with hummus, pita chips and vegetable sticks.

The consumption of yogurt is associated with a reduced risk of weight gain and cardiovascular disease. Rich in protein, calcium and beneficial bacteria, yogurt is an ingredient that must be included as a part of everyday meals.

CALORIES (KCAL)	PROTEIN	FATS	CARBOHYDRATES	FIBRE
117.9	3.5	3.8	18.6	3.8

(per serving)

Fire-Roasted Pumpkin Chutney

The inspiration for this recipe came from the pumpkins harvested from our little pumpkin patch over one season. When I shared pictures of the pumpkins roasting over an open fire, I was told that this method is common in a Bengali preparation of this vegetable. Vegetable chutneys like this one can be mixed into some steamed rice along with a spoonful of ghee to make a quick and satisfying meal.

MAKES
1½ cups (approx.)

250 g yellow/red pumpkin wedge
A few drops of oil
3 green chillies
½ a lemon, juiced
¾ tsp salt

THE SEASONING
1 tbsp mustard oil
½ tsp grated fresh ginger
1 clove garlic, crushed

1 Place the whole wedge of pumpkin – peel, pith, seeds and all – on the largest burner of your gas stove. Roast for a good 20–25 minutes. The peel will char and the edges of the pumpkin will turn black and acquire charred spots. The flesh won't be cooked through though.

2 To cook the flesh, place some water in a pressure cooker. Now pick up the entire wedge of charred pumpkin with a pair of sturdy tongs and place it in a container that will fit inside the pressure cooker. Put the container in and close the pressure cooker with the lid and the pressure weight plugged in.

3 When it reaches full pressure (first whistle) turn off the heat. Open the cooker after the pressure subsides. The pumpkin flesh will now be soft and 'scoopable'.

4 Poke a knife into the pumpkin flesh to steady the wedge and use a tablespoon to scrape out the seeds and pith. Discard.

5 Using the same spoon, scoop out all the flesh, right up to the skin into a medium-sized bowl. Discard the leftover skin and burnt sides. You'll get around 1 cup of creamy pumpkin puree with a lovely smoky aroma.

6 Apply a little oil on the green chillies and char them on an open flame for around 30 seconds.

7 Slit them open, scrape out the pith and seeds and discard.

8 Roughly chop the flesh and mash it along with the pumpkin.

9 Season with salt.

THE SEASONING

1 Heat the mustard oil in a small pan or tempering ladle till almost smoking.

2 Add the ginger and garlic.

TO SERVE

1 Pour the tempering over the prepared chutney. Mix it well and transfer into a bowl.

2 Serve with steamed rice and ghee or rotis.

You can also try the same recipe with a large aubergine that is used for making bharta.

Pumpkin has phenolic antioxidants that prevent cellular damage induced by high blood sugar. Even though it is considered a 'high sugar' vegetable, diabetic patients benefit from including a portion of dark-yellow pumpkin in their diet.

CALORIES (KCAL)	PROTEIN	FATS	CARBOHYDRATES	FIBRE
281.7	2.4	20.1	23.1	6.3

(per serving)

Baked Zucchini Pasta

Zucchini noodles are the best alternative to noodles or pasta. Zucchini's mild taste is a ready canvas for any flavour. From hakka noodles to pad thai to aglio olio spaghetti, zucchini noodles are up for any adventure. Try this healthier version of a baked pasta dish for a quick weeknight dinner.

SERVES 2–3

2 medium-sized green zucchini

THE SAUCE

4–6 ripe tomatoes
1 tbsp olive oil
6–7 cloves garlic, finely chopped
1 small onion, finely chopped
¾ tsp salt, divided as specified
1 tsp dried Italian herbs, crushed
1 tbsp tomato paste

TO PREPARE

1 Using a sharp peeler, peel fine strips along the length of the zucchini.

2 Place the zucchini strips in a microwave-safe bowl. Cover and microwave on high for 1 minute.

THE SAUCE

1 Blanch the tomatoes by leaving them in boiling hot water for 5 minutes.

2 Drain and peel the tomatoes. Finely chop.

3 Heat the oil in a pan. Over moderate heat sauté the garlic for a few seconds.

4 Add the onion with a pinch of salt and sauté on medium flame for 5–6 minutes or until translucent.

5 Add the tomatoes, the remaining salt and the herbs.

6 Keep stirring over high heat till the tomatoes collapse into a sauce.

7 Simmer for a good 10 minutes, adding the tomato paste towards the end. Mix well.

THE VEGETABLES

½ tbsp olive oil

2 handfuls chopped vegetables (mushrooms or bell peppers)

THE TOPPINGS

2 tbsp grated mozzarella cheese

¼ tsp smoked paprika

THE VEGETABLES

1 Sauté the vegetables you plan to use in this dish in ½ tbsp olive oil till partially softened or cooked.

TO FINISH

1 Preheat the oven to 180°C.

2 Arrange the zucchini strips in a baking dish.

3 Top with half of the tomato sauce.

4 Arrange a layer of veggies on top of the sauce and then add the remaining tomato sauce.

5 Sprinkle the cheese and smoked paprika as the top layer.

6 Place the baking dish in the centre of the preheated oven and bake for 15 minutes. Serve hot. (This dish is perfect for days when you've over-indulged with other meals.)

You can use lasagne sheets instead of zucchini strips. You can also use thin slices of aubergine. This is a good recipe for a potluck lunch or dinner. Double or triple the ingredient quantities and you will have enough to fill a large baking tray and feed a small crowd.

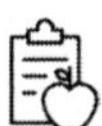

Using zucchini noodles (zoodles as they are popularly called) cuts down the calories in a pasta dish by 90 per cent. When tossed in tomato sauce or pesto, one hardly misses the real spaghetti.

CALORIES (KCAL)	PROTEIN	FATS	CARBOHYDRATES	FIBRE
135.2	5.9	7.6	11.5	3.5

(per serving)

Jewelled Salad

Vegetables and fruits with jewel tones come together in a bowl with a bit of South-Indian tadka (tempering) to make this jewelled salad. An upgraded version of a *koshimbir*, this salad lends vibrancy to any Indian meal.

SERVES 4

THE SALAD

1 sweetcorn cob or ¾ cup frozen corn kernels
¼ cup green peas
1 medium-sized cucumber
3–4 slices pineapple
½ cup pomegranate arils
¼ cup grated raw mango
2–3 tbsp grated coconut
2 lemons, juiced
1 tsp salt, divided

THE TEMPERING

2 tsp coconut oil
½ tsp mustard seeds
½ tsp cumin seeds (jeera)

THE GARNISH

1 tsp fresh coriander leaves, very finely chopped

THE SALAD

1 Shuck the sweet corn over a large bowl. Transfer the sweetcorn kernels (fresh or frozen) to a microwave-safe glass bowl with ½ cup water and ½ tsp salt.

2 Cover with a lid and microwave on high for 3 minutes.

3 Drain and keep aside to cool.

4 Place the green peas (fresh or frozen) in a microwave-safe bowl with ½ cup of water and microwave on high for 3–5 minutes or till the green peas are tender.

5 Drain and keep aside to cool.

6 Peel the cucumber. Cut it lengthwise in half. Scoop out the seeds and discard. Chop the flesh into small pieces.

7 Dice the pineapple slices, keeping the size similar to the cucumber.

8 Mix the corn, green peas, cucumber, pineapple, pomegranate arils, mango and coconut in a large bowl.

9 Combine the lemon juice with ½ tsp salt in a small cup and pour it over the ingredients in the bowl. Toss well.

THE TEMPERING

1 Heat the coconut oil in a small pan over moderate heat.

2 Add the mustard seeds and cumin seeds.

3 Once the seeds start spluttering, pour the contents of the pan over the salad and toss well.

TO SERVE

1 Garnish with coriander leaves and serve at room temperature.

You can add 1 ½ cups of yogurt to this salad to make a colourful raita *that can be served with a pulao or biryani.*

CALORIES (KCAL)	PROTEIN	FATS	CARBOHYDRATES	FIBRE
142.0	2.7	7.8	17.1	4.4

(per serving)

Roasted Beetroot and Corn Salad

While I am vehemently against corn making an appearance in every single vegetarian dish in restaurants, I am partial to this beetroot and corn salad. Be it the contrasting colours on the plate, or the fun texture added from the bites of corn, this is a winning combination. If you haven't roasted beetroots before, trust me, from now on this will be your favourite way to deal with them.

SERVES 2

2 medium-sized beetroots
1 apple
¾ cup corn kernels, fresh or frozen
2 pinches of salt
½ cup baby salad greens

THE DRESSING

½ tsp mustard powder
½ tsp red chilli powder
2 tbsp extra-virgin olive oil
1 tsp apple cider vinegar
½ tsp salt

THE SALAD

1 Preheat an air fryer/OTG/oven to 190°C.

2 Poke holes in the beetroots using a sharp knife or knitting needles. Wrap them in two layers of aluminium foil.

3 Roast the beetroots in the preheated air fryer for 20 minutes. Alternatively, place the beetroots in the centre of the preheated OTG or oven and roast for 35 minutes.

4 Remove and keep aside till cool enough to handle. Then tug off the peels and discard.

5 Cut the beetroots lengthwise in half and then into very thin slices. Keep aside.

6 Place the corn kernels with ½ cup water and 2 pinches of salt in a microwave-safe bowl.

7 Cover and microwave on high for 3 minutes. You can also cook the corn kernels in a small pan on the stovetop.

8 Cut the apple into thin slices and then into matchsticks, avoiding the core and seeds.

THE DRESSING

1 Whisk all the ingredients for the dressing in a bowl, till smooth and creamy.

TO SERVE

1 Take 2 plates and layer the salad greens, corn, apple and beetroot slices carefully so that the beetroot doesn't dye the rest of the salad pink.

2 Drizzle the salad dressing over the prepared plates.

You can make mustard powder by crushing lightly-toasted black or yellow mustard seeds in a mortar and pestle.

You can also use red/white wine vinegar instead of apple cider vinegar.

CALORIES (KCAL)	PROTEIN	FATS	CARBOHYDRATES	FIBRE
279.1	4.7	16.0	33.8	8.1

(per serving)

Not Your Usual Kachumber Salad

The salad component of an Indian meal tends to be a couple of pieces of chopped cucumber, a green chilli or a smashed onion relegated to the corner of the thali or an onion-tomato-cucumber salad called *kachumber*. My version of this salad has the usual suspects but also a few extra ingredients to make it special. Serve a spoonful to liven up an Indian meal or a larger serving as one of the courses for dinner.

SERVES 4–6

THE SALAD
- 1 large cucumber (approx. 500 g)
- 2 medium-sized tomatoes
- 2 medium-sized onions
- 10–12 cape gooseberries (rasbhari)
- 2 fresh red chillies

THE DRESSING
- 2 tbsp extra-virgin olive oil
- ½ tbsp white wine vinegar
- 1 tbsp honey
- ¼ tsp salt
- Black pepper, freshly ground
- ½ tsp dried thyme leaves
- A pinch of turmeric powder

THE SALAD

1 Peel the cucumber. Cut it lengthwise in half. Scoop out and discard the seeds.

2 Slice each cucumber half into ¼-inch slices.

3 Cut the tomatoes in half and then into ¼-inch slices.

4 Peel the onion and slice similarly.

5 Pull off the parchment-like capes from the gooseberries and discard.

6 Wash the gooseberries and cut into halves.

7 Slice the red chillies at a diagonal.

8 Toss the prepared vegetables, fruit and chillies together in a large bowl.

THE DRESSING

1 Whisk the ingredients for the dressing in a small bowl, till thick and creamy.

TO SERVE

1 Pour the dressing over the salad and toss well.

2 Cover and refrigerate for 1 hour for best results.

See photograph 2 of colour insert.

You can blend this whole salad, dressing and all, in a high-powered blender to make an interesting gazpacho. *Top it with a light drizzle of extra-virgin olive oil before serving.*

If cape gooseberries are not available you can use any seasonal fruit such as mango, peach or watermelon. It is the touch of sweet and sour juiciness that makes all the difference to this salad.

The antioxidant value of cape gooseberries is almost at par with that of blueberries. This bright yellow berry is rich in carotenoids that are vital for good eyesight.

CALORIES (KCAL)	PROTEIN	FATS	CARBOHYDRATES	FIBRE
93.3	1.3	5.0	11.4	1.8

(per serving)

Rainbow Smoothie

The only smoothies my kid will drink are ones with chocolate, peanut butter or banana or all of the above. When this colourful smoothie met with his approval I was delighted! It is the best way to get your kids' (or your own) quota of vitamins and antioxidants in a single glass. By all means, serve them singly, but make all 3 and layer the colours in a glass to make it a smoothie no one can refuse.

SERVES 2

THE YELLOW SMOOTHIE

½ large ripe mango
½" piece fresh turmeric root
4 slices fresh pineapple
¼ cup oats, soaked overnight
½ cup yogurt
2 ice cubes

THE GREEN SMOOTHIE

20 fresh spinach leaves
½ green apple
¼ tsp black pepper, freshly ground
½ cup yogurt
2 ice cubes

THE RED SMOOTHIE

½ cup finely diced beetroot
2 medium-sized carrots, finely sliced
6 strawberries or 1 slice watermelon
½" piece fresh ginger
½ cup yogurt
2 ice cubes

THE YELLOW SMOOTHIE

1 Peel and cube the mango.

2 Peel and slice the turmeric root.

3 Blend all the ingredients until smooth, using 2–3 tbsp of water if needed. (Rinse the blender jar after each smoothie so that the colours don't mix.)

THE GREEN SMOOTHIE

1 Blend all the ingredients until smooth, using 2–3 tbsp of water if needed.

THE RED SMOOTHIE

1 Put the beetroots and carrot with 3–4 tbsp water in a microwave-safe bowl.

2 Cover and microwave on high for 4 minutes.

3 Hull the strawberries and cut into half.

4 If using watermelon, remove and discard the seeds. Cut the flesh into chunks.

5 Blend all the ingredients until smooth, using 2–3 tbsp of water if needed.

1: Rainbow Smoothie

2: Not Your Usual Kachumber Salad

3: Baked Tapioca Chips and Bengal Gram Hummus with Roasted Tomatoes

4: Coriander and Green Apple Chutney

5: Herby Bamboo Rice Salad

6: Baby Aubergines with a Crunchy Spice Mix

7: Barley Soup with Pistou

8: Banana and Buckwheat Pancakes

9: Drumstick Curry

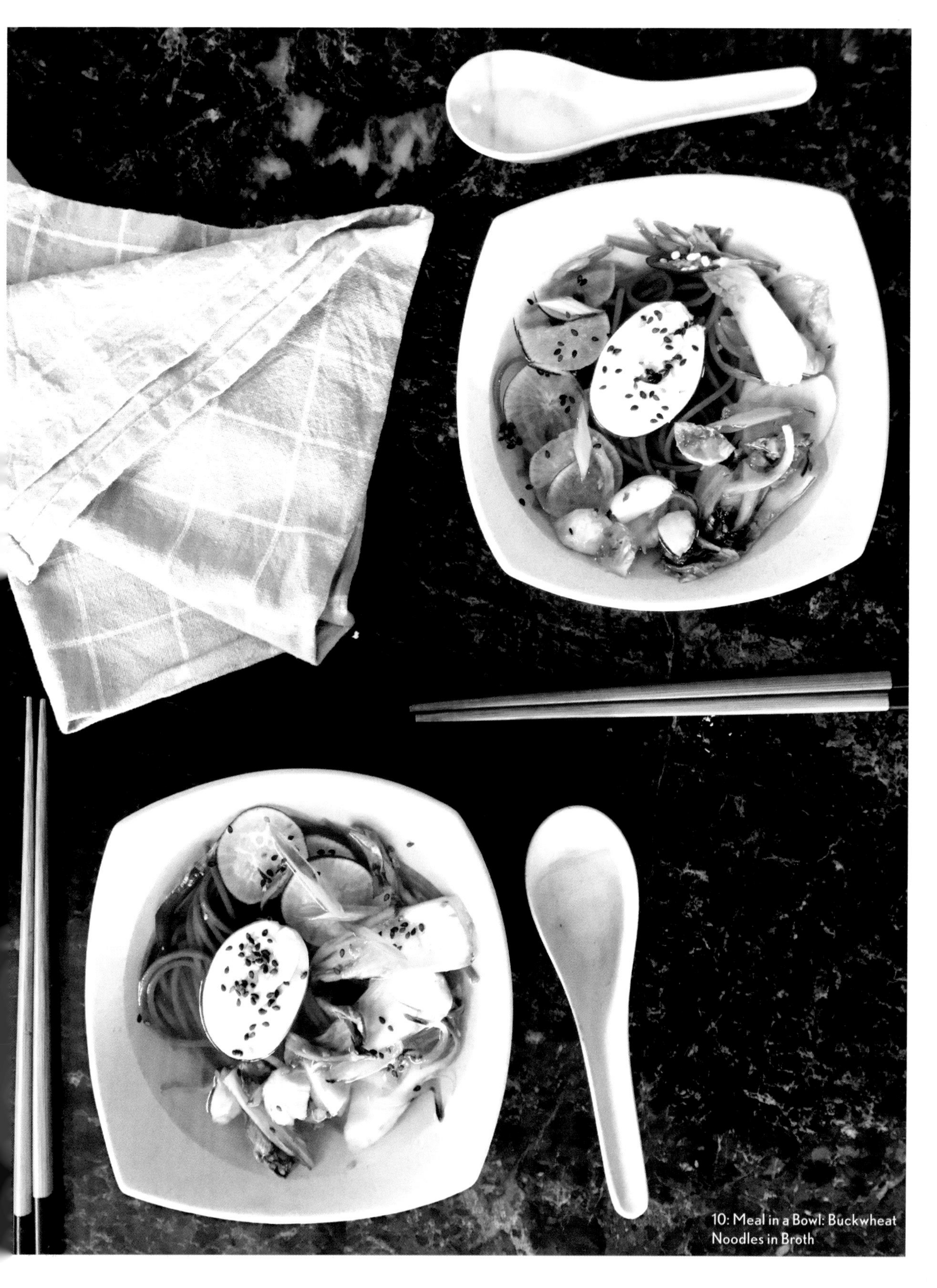

10: Meal in a Bowl: Buckwheat Noodles in Broth

11: Flavour-Bursting Corn Bread

TO LAYER

1 Take two glasses. Pour a quarter of each of the smoothies for each layer.

2 To get proper layers, pour the liquid over a spoon held close to the smoothie level in the glass. You'll get a total of six layers.

3 Serve immediately.

See photograph 1 of colour insert.

To make quick smoothies you can prep and pack ingredients for 1–2 servings in re-sealable plastic bags and freeze. Blend with yogurt in the morning. No need to add extra ice.

You can also store any leftover fruit after smoothie making in re-sealable plastic bags and freeze for another smoothie.

CALORIES (KCAL)	PROTEIN	FATS	CARBOHYDRATES	FIBRE
114.3	4.0	4.0	15.8	3.0

(per serving)

Sprout and Berry Salad

This salad is all about putting together a medley of colours in a bowl. Sprouts are easily available in most supermarkets and this is a good way to use them. Dried cranberries and oranges push this salad towards the sweeter side and those with a sweet tooth will love it. This salad can also be paired with a spicy main-course dish.

SERVES 2

THE SALAD

2 oranges
1 small onion
1 cup mixed sprouts (moong, horse gram/ kulthi)
1 cup finely chopped salad greens
½ cup cranberries, fresh or dried

THE DRESSING

2 tbsp extra-virgin olive oil
1 tsp apple cider vinegar
1 orange, zested
2–3 tbsp fresh orange juice
½ tsp salt

THE SALAD

1. Zest the oranges before using them in the salad.
2. Separate the segments and cut each segment in half. Remove seeds.
3. Peel and finely chop the onion.
4. Mix all the ingredients for the salad in a bowl.

THE DRESSING

1. Whisk together all the dressing ingredients until thick and creamy.

TO SERVE

1. Pour the dressing over the salad and toss well. Serve immediately.

You can add a handful of cooked grains such as millet, quinoa or brown rice to the salad which will make it more filling. Instead of dried cranberries you can use any berries that are in season, such as strawberries or cape gooseberries.

To zest the orange, use a sharp, fine grater to grate the peel just till you reach the white layer.

Sprouting improves the nutritional profile of grains and pulses, especially enzymes, essential amino acids and B vitamins, and decreases overall starch and anti-nutrients such as phytates. Digestibility of protein and starch are also improved.

CALORIES (KCAL)	PROTEIN	FATS	CARBOHYDRATES	FIBRE
256.8	4.3	15.4	27.2	5.1

(per serving)

Cauliflower with Chickpeas

With the arrival of the keto revolution, cauliflower has suddenly become a sought-after vegetable and is being used to make everything from 'rice' to pizza base. This recipe is a delicious twist on the all-time favourite aloo gobhi, but gives more protein bang for the buck.

SERVES 2

THE CAULIFLOWER

1 small cauliflower, broken into florets
1 tsp salt
½ tsp turmeric powder

THE TEMPERING

1 tbsp vegetable oil
1 tsp cumin seeds
A pinch of asafoetida powder (hing)
1 tsp fresh ginger, grated
3 cloves garlic, grated

THE OTHER INGREDIENTS

1 cup chickpeas (kabuli chana), cooked
1 tsp curry powder (subzi masala)
½ tsp turmeric powder
½ tsp red chilli powder
1 tsp salt
½ tsp garam masala powder

THE CAULIFLOWER

1 While cooking cauliflower it is extremely important to ensure that it is thoroughly clean and worm-free. Soak the florets in a bowl of lukewarm water with 1 tsp salt and ½ tsp turmeric powder for 15 minutes. Fish out the florets with a slotted spoon, rinse and keep aside.

2 Half fill a medium-sized pan with water and bring to a boil over high heat. When the water is boiling add the cauliflower florets, lower the heat to moderate and boil for 4–5 minutes.

3 Drain through a colander. Shake off excess water and wipe the florets dry.

THE TEMPERING

1 Heat the oil in a large frying pan. Add the cumin seeds and asafoetida powder.

2 When the seeds splutter, stir in the ginger and garlic. Sauté for 30 seconds.

TO COMPLETE

1 After sautéing the ginger and garlic add the prepared cauliflower and cooked chickpeas.

2 Add all the spice powders except the garam masala powder.

3 Stir in the salt. Toss well to combine.

THE GARNISH

1–2 tbsp fresh coriander leaves, finely chopped

4 Cover and cook over low heat for 5 minutes, sprinkling some water if required.

5 Finish with garam masala powder, giving it a final toss.

TO SERVE

1 Remove into a serving bowl. Garnish with coriander leaves. Serve hot.

You can serve this dish with rotis or jeera rice. This can also be used as a stuffing for grilled sandwiches or quesadillas.

With just 4 grams of carbs per 100-gram serving, cauliflower is everyone's favourite low-carb vegetable. Vegetables such as cabbage, kale, broccoli, Brussels sprouts and cauliflower belong to the Brassica family. Vegetables from this family are protective against cancers.

CALORIES (KCAL)	PROTEIN	FATS	CARBOHYDRATES	FIBRE
251.9	10.5	9.9	32.1	9.4

(per serving)

French Beans with Peanuts

This recipe is a cross between a dry curry and a salad. While in a regular Indian kitchen, French beans find their way into pulao or mixed-vegetable curries, in my family, they go into a dry curry called *usili*, which is one of my all-time favourites.

SERVES 2

250 g tender French beans
½ tsp salt
½ tsp cumin seeds
½ tsp black peppercorns
1 tbsp coconut oil
1 tbsp finely chopped garlic
1 medium-sized onion, finely sliced
½ tsp red chilli flakes

THE GARNISH

¼ cup coarsely crushed roasted peanuts

1 Cut the top and tail of the beans and pull away the fibrous side threads. Slice them diagonally into juliennes.

2 Bring a small pan of water to boil over high heat. Add salt. Keep some iced water handy in a bowl.

3 Once the water is boiling throw in the beans. Boil for 4–5 minutes or till nearly cooked.

4 Drain the beans and plunge them into the bowl of iced water to stop further cooking. This also ensures that they retain a vibrant green colour.

5 Lightly toast the cumin seeds and peppercorns in a small pan for 2 minutes over moderate heat or till aromatic.

6 Remove and keep aside. When cool, crush coarsely in a mortar and pestle.

7 Heat oil in a medium-sized frying pan. Stir in the garlic and onion and sauté for 4–5 minutes.

8 Add the blanched beans to the pan and toss well.

TO SERVE

1 Sprinkle the prepared spice mix and chilli flakes over the beans, give them a quick toss and remove into a shallow serving bowl.

2 Top with the peanuts and serve immediately.

You can try the same recipe with a mix of winter vegetables such as carrots and green peas along with the beans.

French beans offer protection from cancer due to the presence of resistant starch, soluble and insoluble dietary fibre, phenolic compounds and other vital micronutrients.

GARDENING TIP:

French beans come in colours such as yellow and purple in addition to the regular green. If you find these heirloom seeds, try and grow them in pots with 3 bamboo sticks stuck into the soil to make a cone-like support. Keep the pots in a sunny spot. Pluck the beans every 2–3 days during harvest time.

CALORIES (KCAL)	PROTEIN	FATS	CARBOHYDRATES	FIBRE
186.0	6.2	12.0	14.4	4.5

(per serving)

Broccoli and Corn Soup

Two colours are always better than one! The contrasting colours of green and pale yellow in this bowl of soup with a minimal ingredient list are just the sort of thing I find appealing. The best part, in my opinion, is that it tastes great whether it is served hot or served chilled. You can try this all-season soup with a thick slice of crusty bread for company.

SERVES 2

THE BROCCOLI SOUP

1 small head of broccoli (approx. 250 g)
½ tsp + a pinch of salt
200 ml skimmed milk
¼ tsp garlic powder
½ tsp black pepper, freshly ground

THE CORN SOUP

¾ cup sweetcorn kernels, frozen
¼ tsp + a pinch of salt
200 ml skimmed milk
¼ tsp garlic powder

THE GARNISH

A few drops of extra-virgin olive oil (optional)

THE BROCCOLI SOUP

1 Separate the broccoli into small florets, wash and keep aside.

2 Bring a small pan of water to a boil over high heat.

3 Keep some iced water handy in a bowl.

4 Once the water is boiling, add ½ tsp of salt and the broccoli florets. Boil for 2 minutes.

5 Fish out the florets using a slotted spoon and plunge into the bowl of iced water. This ensures that they retain their green colour.

6 Drain the broccoli florets and blend with the milk, a pinch of salt, garlic powder and black pepper, till smooth and creamy.

7 Transfer to a pan.

THE CORN SOUP

1 Place the corn kernels in a microwave-safe bowl. Add ¼ cup water and mix in ¼ tsp salt.

2 Cover and microwave on high for 4–5 minutes, till the corn is cooked.

3 Drain the water and blend the cooked corn kernels with the milk, a pinch of salt and the garlic powder, till smooth and creamy.

4 Transfer to another pan. (Both the soups should have the same consistency.)

TO ASSEMBLE

1 Chill both the soups or bring them to a boil in separate pans.

2 Transfer the soups to 2 jugs.

3 Take two soup bowls (preferably white, to showcase the soup colours best) and holding both the soup jugs, one in each hand, pour simultaneously from two opposite ends of the bowl. Repeat the process for the other soup bowl.

4 Using a toothpick or chopstick make swirls at the border where the green and yellow soups meet to give it a visually pleasing marbled effect.

TO SERVE

1 Garnish with a few drops of extra-virgin olive oil if you like.

2 Serve immediately.

You can try a mix of spinach and broccoli for the green portion of the soup and roasted or cooked yellow pumpkin can be used as a substitute for corn.

CALORIES (KCAL)	PROTEIN	FATS	CARBOHYDRATES	FIBRE
144.6	9.5	1.4	28.0	5.3

(per serving)

Pumpkin Curry with Local Greens

The orange and green colours of this curry remind me of vintage Kanjivaram sarees. I love this curry and have even made it with home-grown pumpkins from the kitchen garden. In fact, we were blessed with over a dozen pumpkins last year, each weighing 3–4 kilograms. I even took one to my family in Mumbai on a flight as checked-in baggage!

SERVES 3–4

THE SEASONING

- 1 tbsp mustard oil
- 1 tsp fresh ginger, grated
- 1 tbsp garlic, finely chopped
- 4 mild green chillies, slit lengthwise
- A pinch of asafoetida powder (hing)
- 1 medium-sized onion, sliced (approx. 50 g)

THE VEGETABLES

- 2–3 cups roughly chopped local greens (bathua, amaranth, Malabar spinach etc.)
- 2 cups diced red pumpkin
- 1 tsp salt
- 2 tsp curry powder (such as Kitchen King or subzi masala)
- ½ tsp garam masala powder

THE SEASONING

1 Heat the mustard oil in a large frying pan till oil is smoking hot.

2 Reduce the heat. Add the ginger, garlic and green chillies.

3 Fry for a few seconds and then add the asafoetida powder.

4 Add the onion and sauté for 4–5 minutes, till translucent.

THE VEGETABLES

1 Add the leafy greens to the above-made seasoning and toss over high heat, till they start wilting.

2 Stir in the pumpkin.

3 Season with salt, sprinkle curry powder and stir well to combine.

4 Reduce the heat and add 2–3 tbsp of water.

5 Cover and steam cook for 6–7 minutes, or till the pumpkin is cooked through.

TO SERVE

1 Finish with a sprinkling of garam masala powder. Mix well.

2 Serve hot with rotis or dal and rice.

You can use a neutral-flavoured oil but it is best to use mustard oil as it adds a punch of flavour to the curry. Additionally, fenugreek leaves (methi) pair well with the mild sweetness of the pumpkin in this curry.

The bright yellow-orange colour of pumpkin indicates that it is rich in beta-carotene, a precursor to vitamin A, which is essential for good eye health. Eating a meal of this pumpkin curry and greens with roti also keeps you full for longer due to the overall high fibre content.

CALORIES (KCAL)	PROTEIN	FATS	CARBOHYDRATES	FIBRE
73.2	2.3	4.2	7.2	1.3

(per serving)

Coriander and Green Apple Chutney

While coriander chutney needs neither an introduction nor a recipe, this version of the green chutney will be your new favourite. The addition of green apple adds tart and sweet notes that will make people wonder about the secret ingredient.

MAKES ½ cup

- ½ large green apple
- 2 cups fresh coriander leaves (tender stems may be included)
- 2 tbsp peanuts, roasted
- 1–2 green chillies, roughly chopped
- ½ tsp fresh ginger, sliced
- A pinch of turmeric powder
- ½ tsp salt

1 Roughly chop the green apple, discarding the core and seeds. There is no need to peel the apple.

2 Combine all the ingredients in a blender/mixer jar and add 2–3 tbsp of water. Blend till you get a smooth puree.

3 Remove into an airtight jar and refrigerate. This chutney will keep for 3–4 days after which it may start browning.

See photograph 4 of colour insert.

Instead of green apple, you can also use red apple and 1 tsp of lemon juice.

It also makes a lively accompaniment to grilled vegetables or can be had as a part of a grain bowl or a Buddha bowl (a combination of cooked grains, beans, veggies, greens, etc. eaten from a bowl).

Pectin is abundant in apples, a natural fibre found in plant-based foods. Pectin-rich foods help lower cholesterol and are a good choice for diabetic patients. An apple with its peel intact has double the fibre and 40 per cent more vitamin A than a peeled one.

CALORIES (KCAL)	PROTEIN	FATS	CARBOHYDRATES	FIBRE
75.7	1.8	3.0	11.9	3.2

(per ½ serving)

Drumstick Curry

I must admit that there is no elegant way to present or eat a dish made with drumsticks. But I can guarantee that there is so much flavour in every bite of this rustic dish that you will soon be adding drumsticks to your weekly veggie shopping list. Many Indian communities have recipes that use drumsticks, especially Goan, Odia and Andhra cuisines. This recipe, though, is my own creation.

SERVES 2

- 3 drumsticks
- 1 tsp fennel seeds (saunf)
- ½ tsp carom seeds (ajwain)
- 1 tbsp groundnut oil
- 2 green chillies, slit lengthwise
- 1 tsp grated fresh ginger
- 4–5 cloves garlic, finely minced
- 1 bay leaf
- 1 medium-sized onion, sliced (approx. 50 g)
- ¾ tsp salt, divided
- 3 tbsp fresh coconut, grated
- 1 tsp tamarind paste
- 1 tbsp crushed jaggery
- ½ tsp turmeric powder
- ½ tsp red chilli powder (optional)

THE GARNISH

- 2 tbsp fresh coconut, grated

1 Lightly peel the drumsticks, especially if they seem to have a thick skin. Cut into 1½-inch-sized batons. Keep aside.

2 Heat a small fry pan.

3 Add the fennel seeds and carom seeds and toss for a few seconds, or till aromatic. Remove and keep aside.

4 Heat the oil in a large frying pan. Fry the green chillies, ginger, garlic and bay leaf for 1 minute over moderate heat.

5 Add the onion and a pinch of salt and cook for 4–5 minutes till translucent. Mix in all the remaining ingredients along with the drumstick pieces and toss over high heat for a few seconds.

6 Pour in ¾ cup of water. Cover and cook over moderate heat till the drumsticks are tender but firm. Cooking time depends on the thickness and freshness of the drumsticks.

7 You can pick one out and mash it with your thumb to check for readiness. At this point the masala will be clinging to the cooked drumstick pieces.

TO SERVE

1 Remove into a dish and garnish with some more fresh coconut.

2 Serve hot with rotis or steamed rice.

See photograph 9 of colour insert.

An important factor that accounts for the medicinal uses of the Moringa oleifera *(drumstick) plant is its very wide range of vital antioxidants, antibiotics and nutrients including vitamins and minerals. Almost all parts of the* Moringa *plant can be used as a source of nutrition with other useful values.*

In 2008, to commemorate Earth Day, the National Institutes of Health named the drumstick tree as the 'Botanical of the Year', adding that 'perhaps like no other single species, this plant has the potential to help reverse multiple major environmental problems and provide for many unmet human needs.'

CALORIES (KCAL)	PROTEIN	FATS	CARBOHYDRATES	FIBRE
211.6	2.5	16.7	13.9	5.4

(per serving)

Mango Arugula Salad

Fleshy, juicy, sweet mangoes like *banganapalli* or *mallika* work best in this salad but if you are a sworn *alphonso* loyalist, then by all means use that. The coming together of sweet mangoes, crunchy croutons, punchy arugula, salty blue cheese and fiery red chillies will have your taste buds tingling with glee. I must add that it is a visual feast too. Do not let the mango season get away without trying out this salad.

SERVES 2

- 2 slices whole-grain bread (2–3 days old)
- 1 tsp olive oil
- ½ tsp mixed dried herbs of choice
- 200 g mango cubes or 1 large ripe mango
- 2 handfuls of arugula leaves
- ½ cup fresh mint leaves
- 50 g blue cheese
- 1 fresh red chilli
- 1 tbsp extra-virgin olive oil
- Pink salt for grinding (or any other coarse salt)

1 Preheat the oven to 180°C.

2 Tear the bread into bite-sized pieces.

3 Combine the oil and dried herbs in a bowl and toss the bread cubes in this. Layer the bread cubes on a lined baking tray.

4 Place the tray in the centre of the preheated oven and bake for 5 minutes, till the bread is light brown and crisp. (This can also be done in an air fryer if you use one.)

5 Peel and dice the mango into bite-sized pieces. Take roughly 200 g of mango cubes (100 g per serving).

6 Take 2 serving bowls or plates. Make a bed of arugula and mint leaves.

7 Top with mango chunks and croutons.

8 Crumble the blue cheese on top.

9 Snip the red chilli into fine slices over the salad.

10 Drizzle extra-virgin olive oil and finish with a couple of grinds of pink salt or any other coarse salt.

11 Serve immediately before the croutons get soggy.

See photograph 26 of colour insert.

Can diabetics eat mangoes? The answer to this very commonly-asked question is possibly yes: eating ½ a cup of chopped mango in a salad or along with a meal with low glycaemic index or a protein-rich meal will not affect blood sugar levels drastically. Talk to your doctor or nutritionist on how to include this seasonal fruit in your meal plans. Portion control is essential, though.

CALORIES (KCAL)	PROTEIN	FATS	CARBOHYDRATES	FIBRE
256.4	10.0	14.8	21.1	4.6

(per serving)

Baby Aubergines with a Crunchy Spice Mix

While growing up I heartily disliked aubergines. Eating them would make my mouth itch so I assumed I was allergic and that ensured that my family kept it away from me for the longest time. But when I started cooking with aubergines I realized that some varieties didn't bother me. I guess growing up means starting to like the very foods you hated as a child. This curry is one of the popular ways to cook small aubergines in Tamil cuisine. It goes very well with rice and *mor kuzhambu*, a Tamil curry made with yogurt.

SERVES 2

THE AUBERGINES

6 small aubergines (baingan) (approx. 200 g)
1 tbsp groundnut oil
1 sprig fresh curry leaves
¼ tsp turmeric powder
½ tsp salt

THE SPICE MIX (PODI)

½ tsp oil
2 dried red chillies
1½ tbsp husked, split Bengal gram (chana dal)
1 tbsp husked, split black gram (urad dal)
½ tsp cumin seeds
1 tsp coriander seeds
1 flake tamarind
1 tsp fennel seeds (saunf)
2 tbsp desiccated coconut

THE AUBERGINES

1 Slice off the tops of the aubergines and discard.

2 Cut the aubergines in half lengthwise and cut each half into ¼-inch thick slices.

3 Heat the oil in a medium-sized frying pan.

4 Strip the curry leaves off the stem and add them to the hot oil.

5 Once they splutter, add the aubergines, turmeric powder and salt. Stir well over high heat for 1–2 minutes.

6 Lower the heat to sim and keep covered with a lid for 6–8 minutes, allowing the aubergines to cook through.

THE SPICE MIX (PODI)

1 Heat the oil in a small frying pan over moderate heat.

2 Add all the ingredients except the coconut.

3 Keep stirring over moderate heat till the dals turn golden brown.

4 Add the coconut and stir for another 2–3 minutes till it turns light golden and aromatic.

5 Remove from heat and allow it to cool for 5 minutes.

6 In a mixer jar, pulse this mixture till you get a coarse powder.

TO COMPLETE

1 Measure out 2 tbsp of the freshly prepared spice mix and sprinkle it over the cooked aubergines in the pan.

2 Cover and cook for 2–3 minutes.

3 Spoon the aubergines into a serving bowl.

4 Serve hot with rice and *rasam.*

See photograph 6 of colour insert.

You can store the remaining podi in an airtight container in the refrigerator for up to a week. It can be used to prepare similar dishes with bell peppers, cabbage or potatoes.

CALORIES (KCAL)	PROTEIN	FATS	CARBOHYDRATES	FIBRE
139.9	3.0	9.6	12.1	5.9

(per serving)

Petha Curry

Ash gourd (petha), the large white pumpkin, is used in Tamil and Kerala cuisine to make *avial*, a popular coconut-based curry. It is also used in *kootu*, a preparation that combines it with dal and a spice paste. In this recipe I have used ash gourd with greens and cooked Bengal gram (kala chana) to prepare a hearty curry that you can serve with rice or rotis.

SERVES 3–4

- 1 tbsp groundnut oil
- 2 green chillies, cut lengthwise
- ¼ tsp fenugreek seeds
- ½ tsp cumin seeds
- A pinch of asafoetida powder (hing)
- 1 medium-sized tomato, roughly chopped
- ½ tsp turmeric powder
- ¾ tsp salt, divided
- 2½ cups ash gourd (approx. 250 g), diced (1" dice)
- 2 cups Malabar spinach (poi), loosely packed
- A generous ½ cup cooked whole Bengal gram (kala chana)
- 1 tsp chole masala
- 2 tsp rice flour

1 Heat the oil in a 3–4 litre pressure cooker over moderate heat.

2 Add the green chillies, fenugreek seeds and cumin seeds.

3 When the seeds splutter, stir in the asafoetida powder, tomato, turmeric powder and a pinch of salt.

4 Sauté over high heat for 1 minute till the tomatoes start breaking down.

5 Add the ash gourd, Malabar spinach and cooked chana along with the chole masala. Stir for another minute.

6 Pour in 1 cup of water and bring to a simmer.

7 Mix the rice flour in 2–3 tbsp of water and stir it into the simmering curry.

8 Season with the remaining salt.

9 Close the pressure cooker with the lid and the pressure weight plugged in.

10 Turn off the heat when the cooker reaches full pressure (first whistle). Open the cooker after the pressure subsides.

11 Remove into a serving bowl and serve hot with rice or rotis.

See photograph 30 of colour insert.

You can prep in advance for this recipe by pressure-cooking the Bengal gram in a separate compartment while cooking rice, dal or anything else. The Bengal gram can then be refrigerated and cooked for dinner or on the following day.

Malabar spinach is called poi saag *in Hindi and is easily available in any local vegetable market. You can substitute it with regular spinach or any other local seasonal greens.*

Ash gourd has a very low carbohydrate content (1.9 grams per 100-gram serving). If you are on a low-carb diet, this vegetable makes a good addition to soups and curries.

CALORIES (KCAL)	PROTEIN	FATS	CARBOHYDRATES	FIBRE
119.8	4.2	4.6	15.8	5.5

(per serving)

Macrobiotic Salad

In macrobiotic salads or pressed salads, the finely sliced vegetables are salted/seasoned and then pressed down with a weighted object for an hour or so. The cured vegetables take on a unique texture, which is somewhere between raw and cooked. This is great for vegetables like radish and beetroot that some people do not like to eat raw.

SERVES 2

THE SALAD

2 European cucumbers
4 round red radishes
1 medium-sized onion
1 celery stalk
½ a lemon
Pink salt and black pepper, coarsely ground, to taste

THE GARNISH

1 tsp black/white sesame seeds, toasted

THE SALAD

1 Finely slice the cucumbers and radish.

2 Cut the onion in half and slice into half-moons.

3 Finely slice the celery stalk.

4 Combine the sliced vegetables in a bowl.

5 Squeeze lemon juice over the veggies and season with salt and pepper.

6 Rub the seasoning well into the vegetables using a fair amount of pressure with the fingertips.

7 Place a flat dish, directly over the vegetables and something heavier like a mortar and pestle on top of the dish to apply more pressure.

8 Let this sit on the countertop for an hour or so.

9 Squeeze the briny water out of the vegetables and transfer them to a serving bowl.

TO SERVE

1 Top with toasted sesame seeds and serve immediately.

European or English cucumbers are a smaller-sized cucumber with few or no seeds and can be eaten with the peel. They are available in many supermarkets.

You can also use thicker green leafy vegetables, which are otherwise difficult to eat raw, such as kale or Swiss chard in this salad. Add cooked grains like red rice, millet or quinoa to turn this light salad into a heartier one.

The salt cures or partly cooks the vegetables, preserving the active live enzymes while making them more digestible. The slight fermentation of the vegetables also gives us the benefit of probiotics or beneficial gut bacteria.

CALORIES (KCAL)	PROTEIN	FATS	CARBOHYDRATES	FIBRE
47.0	1.1	1.0	9.6	1.9

(per serving)

Granny's Digestive Shot

After a Tamil wedding lunch, betel leaves with betel nuts and lime would be served on a tray around which all the adults would sit, chewing on the betel leaves and dissecting the various dishes that had been served for lunch with a side of the latest family gossip. As kids we would love to sneak away a leaf or two when the adults weren't watching. Chewing on the leaf would make our tongues burn and it felt like an adventure. This was why we weren't allowed to eat it in the first place but forbidden food is always more fun to eat, right?

This digestive shot is a home remedy that relieves digestion-related symptoms such as nausea and bloating. It has betel leaf as its main ingredient and a smattering of other herbs and spices that give digestion a shot in the arm.

MAKES 2 SHOTS

- 2 large betel leaves (paan)
- 3 sprigs fresh mint leaves
- 4 sprigs fresh tender curry leaves
- 1" piece fresh ginger
- ¼ tsp carom seeds (ajwain)
- ½ tsp fennel seeds (saunf)
- A pinch of rock salt
- ½ cup water

1 Coarsely chop the betel leaves. Strip the mint and curry leaves off their stalks. Peel and slice the ginger.

2 Combine all the ingredients except the salt in a small mixer jar. Add water.

3 Close the mixer and blend till the leaves and seeds have turned into a coarse puree.

4 Use a fine sieve and filter out the juice into a small pan. Press down on the solids with the back of a spoon to extract every last drop of juice.

5 Stir in the rock salt.

6 Divide this between two shot glasses and drink immediately.

You can give this to older kids (6+ to be safe) but only after dilution. To dilute, mix 1 tbsp juice with 2–3 tbsp of water, add some honey and make them gulp it down.

A little trivia about betel leaves: A study done with betel-leaf extract and its active constituent eugenol showed that it possessed anti-atherogenic properties, i.e. the ability to reduce cholesterol deposits in the arteries, possibly due to its antioxidant properties. These heart-shaped leaves also possess anti-cancer, anti-bacterial and antioxidant properties.

CALORIES (KCAL)	PROTEIN	FATS	CARBOHYDRATES	FIBRE
2.3	0.1	0.1	0.3	0.2

(per shot)

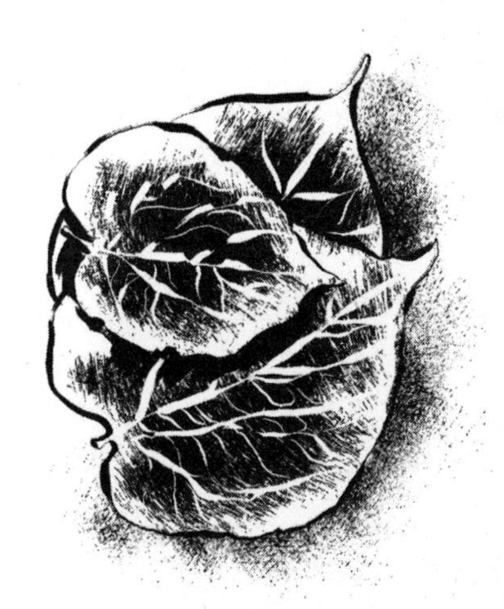

Granny's Herbal Tea Remedy for the Sniffles

If you, like me, are trying to wean yourself off multiple cups of tea and coffee during the day, this herbal tea is the perfect pick-me-up. While this recipe makes 2 teacups, you can prepare a litre in the morning, fill it into a thermos and keep sipping on it through the day. Rainy days and my granny's herbal tea are made for each other. And, yes, herbs and spices used in this do help with the sniffles. That squeeze of lemon provides you with shot of vitamin C.

MAKES 2 TEACUPS

THE TEA

½ cup tulsi leaves (holy basil)
½ tsp black peppercorns
1" piece fresh ginger
A pinch of turmeric powder or a slice of fresh turmeric root
2¼ cup water

TO SERVE

½ a lemon
2 tsp honey

THE TEA

1 Put 2¼ cups of water in a small pan.

2 Tear the tulsi leaves into smaller pieces.

3 Lightly crush the peppercorns in a mortar and pestle.

4 Add the tulsi and pepper to the water in the pan.

5 Peel the ginger. Roughly slice up the root. Pound the slices lightly in a mortar and pestle and add to the water.

6 Stir in the turmeric.

7 Put the pan over high heat and bring the water to a boil.

8 Once it is boiling, lower the heat and allow it to simmer for 5 minutes.

TO SERVE

1 Filter out the tea into two teacups. Finish with a squeeze of lemon and stir in the honey.

2 Drink it warm.

The scientific name for tulsi is Ocimum sanctum Linn *and its active constituent is the phytochemical eugenol which has a positive impact on the immune system. Research has also shown that eugenol has anti-diabetic, pain-relieving and liver-protective properties.*

CALORIES (KCAL)	PROTEIN	FATS	CARBOHYDRATES	FIBRE
17.5	0.2	0.0	4.3	0.2

(per cup)

good carbs

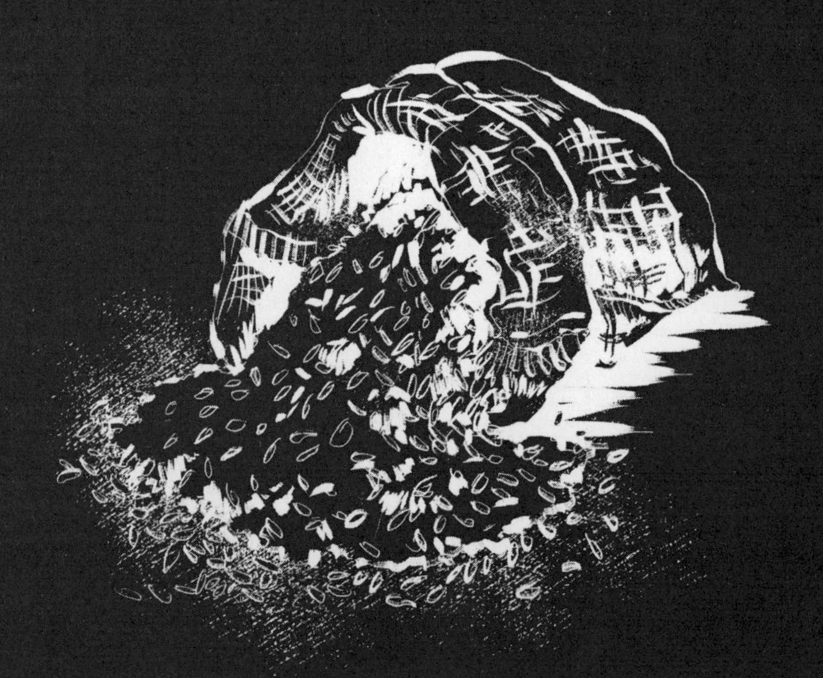

Ask anyone what their comfort food is and, more often than not, you will find carbs featured on that list. For instance, a bowl of steaming hot rice with sambar and ghee is the kind of food my soul craves when I'm feeling down. Consumption of carbs leads to the production of serotonin, a feel-good chemical that elevates our mood, which is one of the reasons why carbs are so beloved.

It is also the food group most people are quick to cut out of their lives in their quest for weight loss. That perception is quite right when it comes to one kinds of carbs – the refined variety. Foods made from refined flours or containing added sugars do nothing for our health, but add empty calories. There is no place for refined carbohydrates in a healthy lifestyle.

On the other hand, there's a world of good carbs, or complex carbohydrates, that are rich in vitamins, minerals and fibre, and come with a host of health benefits. Complex carbohydrates get converted to sugar at a much slower rate in the body compared to refined carbs. Root vegetables, whole grains and pseudo grains like millet, amaranth, buckwheat and quinoa are some of the foods that fall in this category.

Being fibre-rich, these foods have a better satiety factor. They keep you feeling full for longer, even if the quantity consumed is less, thereby aiding weight loss. Carbs containing soluble fibre, such as oats, barley, fruits (with skin), beans help reduce LDL (bad cholesterol). Eating whole grains also improves HDL (good cholesterol), making them an important addition to a heart-friendly diet. The fibre in the carbs ensures a steady rise in blood sugar (as opposed to the rapid spikes from processed refined carbohydrates), which also makes them diabetic-friendly.

It is important for adults to consume around 25–35 grams of fibre in a day, and consuming complex carbohydrates contributes readily to fulfil this requirement. Replacing half of all the grains consumed daily with whole grains is a good start.

In this section, you will find complex carbs for every meal – from overnight oats with caramelized apples for breakfast; salads like the herby bamboo rice salad and root vegetable salad for lunch; anytime snacks like homemade gourmet popcorn; and hearty mains like Thai curried millets and brown rice with spinach and chickpeas for dinner.

Curried Millets with Tofu Crumble

Limiting millets to the role of rice substitutes is totally underestimating their culinary potential. I love using them in salads, appetizers, food bowls and more. Cooked in a flavour-enriched coconut milk gravy and served with crumbled tofu, this hearty meal will turn into one of your favourites.

SERVES 3

THE GREEN CURRY PASTE

1 tbsp coriander seeds
½ tbsp cumin seeds (jeera)
6 cloves garlic, roughly chopped
1" piece galangal root, roughly chopped
10 shallots or Madras onions, roughly chopped
6 green chillies, roughly chopped
A small handful of fresh Thai basil, roughly chopped
1 lemon grass stalk, roughly chopped
A few kaffir lime leaves, roughly chopped
A handful of fresh coriander stems, roughly chopped

THE MILLETS

1 tbsp coconut oil
1 cup coconut milk

THE GREEN CURRY PASTE

1 Toast the coriander and cumin seeds over moderate heat in a small pan till fragrant.

2 Remove from heat and keep aside. Let cool.

3 Blend all the ingredients for the green curry paste in a food processor, using up to ¼ cup of water, till you get a smooth puree.

THE MILLETS

1 Heat the coconut oil in a medium-sized frying pan with a lid over moderate heat.

2 Fry 3 tbsp of the prepared green curry paste in the oil for 2–3 minutes till aromatic. Add the coconut milk and 1 cup of water. Bring to a simmer.

3 Drain the millets and add to the pan. Add salt. Stir well.

4 Cover and cook for 8–10 minutes, till the grains are cooked. Fluff the grains with a fork. Cover and keep aside.

THE TOFU CRUMBLE

1 Heat the oil in a pan over low to moderate heat.

2 Fry 2 tbsp of the prepared curry paste for 2–3 minutes.

3 Add the crumbled tofu.

1 cup foxtail millet (kangnee), soaked for 30 minutes
¾ tsp salt

THE TOFU CRUMBLE

1 tbsp coconut oil
200 g tofu, crumbled
½ tsp salt
½ a lemon

THE GARNISH

A few Thai basil leaves, chopped

4 Season with salt and lemon juice.

5 Toss well and remove from heat.

TO SERVE

1 Spoon a portion of the curried millets into 3 bowls and top with a serving of crumbled tofu.

2 Garnish with the Thai basil leaves and serve.

You can substitute ginger for the galangal root. You can also use any grain like barley, red rice, quinoa or couscous to prepare this dish. Adjust cooking time accordingly.

Another option is to use the Thai curry paste which you can buy ready-made in a supermarket. This recipe can be prepared with red or yellow Thai curry paste as well.

Millets are rich in magnesium, which has been shown to reduce the frequency of migraines and lower blood pressure. Tofu is an excellent source of protein for vegans and vegetarians, providing all the essential amino acids.

CALORIES (KCAL)	PROTEIN	FATS	CARBOHYDRATES	FIBRE
449.9	12.4	28.4	41.1	3.3

(per serving)

Pearl Barley with Mushrooms

This dish brings to you the goodness of whole grains and vegetables with all the sophistication of a main-course dish in a fancy restaurant. Follow this easy recipe as is or get creative by mixing and matching the grains and veggies.

SERVES 2

THE BARLEY

½ cup pearl barley (jau), soaked for 4–6 hours

½ stock cube or 1½ cups home-made vegetable stock

THE MUSHROOMS

¼ tsp unsalted butter or a few drops of olive oil

100 g button mushrooms, halved

A sprinkle of salt

THE OTHER VEGETABLES

1–2 tsp unsalted butter or a few drops of olive oil

1 tbsp finely chopped garlic

1 small onion, sliced

½ a yellow bell pepper, cut into thin strips

¼ cup green peas (fresh or frozen)

THE BARLEY

1 Drain the soaked barley.

2 Put the stock cube in a medium-sized pan with 1½ cups of water; if using homemade vegetable stock, pour it into the pan.

3 Place the pan over high heat and bring the liquid or stock to a boil.

4 Add the drained barley to the boiling stock and boil for 25–30 minutes till the grains are plump and cooked through but still have a bite to them.

5 Remove from heat, drain and keep aside.

THE MUSHROOMS

1 Coat a pan with a little unsalted butter or olive oil and place on high heat.

2 Reduce flame to medium and place the mushrooms in the pan, cut side down.

3 Once this side is golden brown, turn the mushrooms with a pair of tongs to brown the other side as well.

4 Season with a sprinkling of salt, and then remove the mushrooms from the pan and keep aside.

THE OTHER VEGETABLES

1 Add the unsalted butter or olive oil in the same pan and place over moderate heat.

2 Sauté the garlic for a brief period of time till aromatic.

A pinch of salt
½ tsp cumin seeds (jeera), ground

THE SALAD GREENS AND EGGS
2 small handfuls of salad greens, washed and dried
½ tsp extra-virgin olive oil
2 eggs, prepared the way you like them (soft-boiled, hard-boiled, fried, etc.)

3 Add the onion and bell pepper. Cook over moderate heat for 7–8 minutes, till tender.

4 Add the green peas and cook for 4–5 minutes with a pinch of salt and the ground cumin. Turn off the heat.

THE SALAD GREENS

1 Tear the salad greens into bite-sized pieces and toss in extra-virgin olive oil.

TO SERVE

1 Place a layer of greens on each of the two plates.

2 Spoon the cooked barley over the greens.

3 Cover with golden mushrooms and the veggie mix.

4 Top with the eggs.

5 Serve warm.

When you are sautéing mushrooms always ensure that they turn golden-brown before adding salt. Adding salt at the beginning makes them lose water and they stew in their juices.

Instead of barley you can use any other grain of your choice.

100 grams of pearl barley provides 10 grams of protein, besides being a rich source of manganese and selenium. Manganese protects the cells and tissues from free radical damage.

Mushrooms are also a good source of selenium, a mineral which is important for the proper functioning of the thyroid gland.

CALORIES (KCAL)	PROTEIN	FATS	CARBOHYDRATES	FIBRE
278.8	11.4	14.5	24.6	4.8

(per serving)

Wholewheat Pasta with White Bean Mash and Fire-Roasted Veggies

White beans lend heartiness to this pasta dish, while the fire-roasted bell peppers add colour and flavour. This is my go-to recipe when my son asks for a pasta dinner.

SERVES 2

THE BEANS

½ cup white beans, soaked overnight (approx. 100 g)

THE PASTA

200 g wholewheat pasta (fusilli or penne)

THE FIRE-ROASTED VEGETABLES

2 large ripe tomatoes
1 medium-sized red bell pepper

THE SAUCE

1 tbsp olive oil
6 cloves garlic, finely chopped
½ tsp salt
½ tsp black pepper, freshly ground
½ tsp red chilli flakes (optional)
1 tsp dried herbs of choice, crushed

THE BEANS

1 Drain the beans and rinse well.

2 Place them in a pressure cooker with just enough water to cover them.

3 Close the pressure cooker with the lid and the pressure weight plugged in.

4 Cook the beans for 6–7 minutes over low heat after the cooker reaches full pressure (first whistle).

5 Open the cooker after the pressure subsides.

6 Drain the beans and mash coarsely.

7 Keep aside.

THE PASTA

1 Cook the pasta as per the instructions on the pack, taking care to leave it al dente, i.e. with a slight bite to it.

2 Reserve ½ cup of pasta water for later use. Drain the pasta and discard the remaining water.

THE FIRE-ROASTED VEGETABLES

1 Roast the tomatoes and red bell pepper directly over the gas flame of the stove either one by one or simultaneously on 2–3 burners, till completely charred on the outside.

THE GARNISH

A handful of fresh Italian basil

2 tbsp grated Parmesan cheese (optional)

2 Remove from the flame and place in a bowl. Cover and keep aside for 5 minutes till the steam loosens up the skins.

3 Peel the tomatoes and bell pepper.

4 Remove and discard the seeds of the tomatoes.

5 Remove and discard the pith and seeds of the bell pepper.

6 Mash the flesh of the tomatoes and bell pepper with a fork and keep aside.

THE SAUCE

1 Heat the olive oil in a frying pan.

2 Fry the garlic for 30 seconds over moderate heat, till aromatic.

3 Add the mashed, fire-roasted vegetables and fry for a minute.

4 Add the mashed beans and mix well.

5 Thin the sauce with 3–4 tbsp of the reserved pasta water, if needed.

6 Season with salt, pepper, chilli flakes and dried herbs. Stir to combine.

TO SERVE

1 Toss the cooked pasta in the hot sauce.

2 Divide between two plates and garnish with fresh basil and Parmesan.

To prepare a larger quantity of sauce, roast the vegetables in the oven.

Prepare the sauce in advance to pack a quick lunch box in the morning.

You can use any other beans like chickpeas (kabuli chana) or black-eyed peas (lobia), but the mild flavour of these quick cooking beans works best in this pasta recipe.

Roast the vegetables and prepare the sauce while the pasta is being cooked. They will be ready at the same time.

White beans (also called navy beans) provide around 22 grams of protein and over 24 grams of fibre per 100 grams of serving. Including beans in the dish reduces the quantity of pasta consumed, thereby adding more nutrition bang per calorie.

CALORIES (KCAL)	PROTEIN	FATS	CARBOHYDRATES	FIBRE
388.4	17.3	10.4	58.9	13.9

(per serving)

Sweet Potato Paratha

When my kitchen garden goes on a sweet potato rampage, I have the happy problem of plenty. I tackle the sweet potato overload by making every possible dish with this humble, earthy vegetable. My son is a big fan of these parathas. He has them for dinner and then asks me if I can pack the same in his lunch box. As the mashed sweet potato mix is kneaded into the dough, it is easy work for beginner cooks too.

MAKES 4 parathas

THE DOUGH

- 1 large sweet potato (approx. 300 g)
- 1¼ cups wholewheat flour
- ½ tsp grated ginger
- ½ tsp salt
- 2–3 tbsp finely chopped fresh coriander leaves
- 1 tsp raw mango powder (amchoor)
- ½ tsp red chilli powder
- 1 tbsp yogurt
- 1 tsp groundnut oil

THE PARATHAS

- 2 tbsp wholewheat flour
- 1 tbsp ghee or groundnut oil

THE DOUGH

1 Scrub the sweet potato and put it in a pressure cooker. Pour some water into the cooker and pressure cook on high heat until the cooker reaches full pressure (first whistle). Turn off the flame. Open the cooker after the pressure subsides.

2 Peel the sweet potato and mash it.

3 Transfer the mash to a large mixing bowl.

4 Add all the ingredients for the dough, except the oil.

5 Work the flour into the mashed sweet potato and yogurt.

6 Add water 1 tsp at a time, kneading well, till you have a soft, pliable dough.

7 Give the dough a final knead with the oil.

8 Cover and keep aside for 15 minutes.

THE PARATHAS

1 Divide the dough into 4 portions.

2 Roll out each portion into a slightly thick paratha, using dry flour to prevent it from sticking to the surface.

3 Place a tava over moderate heat.

4 When hot, place the rolled paratha on it and cook for 1 minute.

5 Flip the paratha and apply some ghee or oil on the cooked side.

6 Press down on it with a spatula or a round wooden disc. You'll see bubbles forming on the surface, or the paratha may even fluff up fully.

7 Turn it over and apply some more ghee or oil on the other side.

8 Flip and cook for few more seconds.

TO SERVE

1 Remove the paratha from the tava and keep warm in an insulated box or in a kitchen towel till ready to serve.

2 Make the remaining parathas in the same way.

3 Serve with my favourite roasted pineapple chilli chutney (p. 10) or any other accompaniment of your choice.

These parathas are best eaten hot off the tava. If you are packing them for lunch, wrap tightly in foil and pack in an insulated lunch box that will keep the parathas warm.

Sweet potato is a rich source of vitamin A, more specifically carotenoids, providing antioxidant and anti-inflammatory benefits and boosting immunity. Also, those aiming to increase the fibre content of their diet would do well to befriend this root vegetable.

CALORIES (KCAL)	PROTEIN	FATS	CARBOHYDRATES	FIBRE
219.0	5.8	4.0	40.3	6.5

(per paratha)

Wholewheat Pasta with a Two-Minute Magic Sauce

I shared a version of this two-minute pasta sauce on my blog in 2007. This was well before avocado became 'hip'. This recipe went viral in 'those' days, and my readers were amazed to have a pasta sauce recipe that actually used just two ingredients. This is a slightly upgraded version of that sauce.

Whenever life blesses you with a ripe avocado, this is one recipe you must try. Make sure you don't heat the sauce as mashed avocado doesn't respond kindly to cooking.

SERVES 2

150 g wholewheat pasta

THE MAGIC SAUCE

- 2 tbsp sun-dried tomatoes, soaked in warm water for 10 minutes
- ½ a ripe avocado
- ¼ cup fresh or 2 tsp dried oregano leaves
- 1 clove garlic, roughly chopped
- 1 tbsp extra-virgin olive oil

THE GARNISH

- 1 black olive, chopped
- Parmesan cheese, grated

THE PASTA

1 Cook the pasta in a pan of boiling water over high heat as per the instructions on the packet.

2 Wait to prepare the magic sauce till the pasta is almost ready as you don't want the sauce to sit around.

THE MAGIC SAUCE

1 When the pasta is just a minute away from being ready, blend all the ingredients for the sauce in a mixer jar till you get a coarse puree.

TO SERVE

1 Reserve ¼ cup pasta water for later use.

2 Drain the pasta and discard the remaining water.

3 Spoon the sauce into a bowl and toss the pasta in it. Thin it down with 1–2 tbsp of pasta water if needed.

4 Divide between two plates and garnish with the black olive or grated Parmesan cheese.

In the absence of sun-dried tomatoes, you can use 1 tbsp of tomato paste or 3–4 tbsp of tomato puree.

It is very easy to make your own batch of sun-dried tomatoes when the sun is blazing hot. Halve cherry tomatoes and arrange them in a single layer in large plates. Sprinkle with salt and keep in the sun when it is at its peak for 3–4 hours a day. Bring indoors in the evening and keep covered with a mesh at night. Return to the sun on the following day. Depending on the size of the tomatoes and the intensity of the sun, this process will take 5–6 days. Pack in an airtight container or in a jar of extra-virgin olive oil.

For how to get a perfectly ripe avocado: see p. xxvi.

Sun-dried tomatoes are a good source of protein (7.6 grams per cup). They provide calcium along with magnesium and phosphorus, the three minerals required to build strong bones. So, go ahead and let your kids snack on these.

GARDENING TIP:

Bury the avocado seed in a pot of compost enriched soil. Water gently every 2–3 days. In 3–4 weeks you will have an avocado sapling. Even if you can't plant it outdoors, this makes for a pretty houseplant.

CALORIES (KCAL)	PROTEIN	FATS	CARBOHYDRATES	FIBRE
474.5	13.3	21.8	62.7	12.7

(per serving)

Brown Rice with Spinach and Chickpeas

You'll be pleasantly surprised how a handful of ingredients can pack in so much flavour. Cold-pressed coconut oil and garlic work their essence into this simple chickpeas, spinach and rice platter, which makes a good weeknight dinner or lunch box option.

SERVES 4

- 3 cups cooked brown rice, refrigerated overnight
- 3 packed cups spinach leaves
- 1 tbsp coconut oil
- 5 cloves garlic, finely minced
- 1½ cups cooked chickpeas (kabuli chana) (approx. ½ cup dry)
- ½ tsp salt
- 2 tsp sambar powder

1 Remove the rice from the refrigerator.

2 Separate the grains gently, using your fingertips.

3 Roughly chop the spinach leaves.

4 Heat the oil in a large frying pan.

5 Fry the garlic for a few seconds. Don't let it brown.

6 Add the spinach leaves and stir over high heat, till wilted. This will take 20–30 seconds.

7 Throw in the cooked chickpeas and continue to toss over high heat.

8 Lower the heat, add the salt and sambar powder and mix well, till the chickpeas are coated with the seasoning.

9 Add the brown rice and toss gently to combine.

10 Cover with a lid and steam for 3–4 minutes with a sprinkling of water if required. Serve hot.

You'll find details on cooking brown rice in the initial section of the book on p. xxvi.

You can try this recipe with grains like millets or quinoa.

While cooking brown rice or chickpeas, always cook extra portions and refrigerate/ freeze to put together a quick weeknight or lunch box meal. Leftover cooked rice from the refrigerator is the best foil for Chinese-style fried rice.

A little note of warning here: Brown rice has higher levels of arsenic than other grains. It is better to eat this on a rotation with the other whole grains like millets, wheat, quinoa, barley, etc. Also make sure to wash, soak, drain and cook it with fresh, filtered water. If you consume rice for most meals, organic white rice is a better option.

CALORIES (KCAL)	PROTEIN	FATS	CARBOHYDRATES	FIBRE
270.0	9.2	6.2	44.8	6.2

(per serving)

Broken Wheat with Broccoli, Green Peas and Fresh Mint

Broken wheat, also known as dalia, is my favourite replacement for rice, with a dal or sambar. Instead of the time and effort spent in making rotis, you can cook these wheat grains in a variety of dishes. Broken wheat also cooks far more quickly than wholewheat grains. Serve with raita to make a complete meal.

SERVES 2–3

- 1 cup broken wheat (lapsi or dalia)
- 1 tbsp ghee or coconut oil
- 1 bay leaf
- ½ tsp black cumin seeds (shah jeera)
- 3–4 cloves garlic, finely chopped
- 2–3 green chillies, sliced
- 1 small onion, finely chopped
- 8–10 medium-sized broccoli florets (approx. 200 g)
- ¼ cup green peas (frozen is fine)
- A loosely packed ½ cup fresh mint leaves
- ¾ tsp salt

THE GARNISH

- A loosely packed ½ cup fresh mint leaves, roughly chopped

1 Bring 2 cups of water to a boil in a kettle or pan.

2 Wash the broken wheat well. Drain and keep aside.

3 Heat the ghee or oil in a pressure cooker.

4 Fry the bay leaf and cumin seeds for a few seconds.

5 Mix in the garlic, green chillies and onion, and fry over moderate heat for 3–4 minutes.

6 Add the broccoli florets and green peas. Stir to combine with the spices in the cooker.

7 Add the broken wheat and the mint leaves. Fry over moderate heat for 3–4 minutes, till the wheat grains turn somewhat opaque.

8 Season with salt.

9 Add 1¾ cups of boiling water from the kettle. Give it a stir.

10 Close the pressure cooker with the lid and the pressure weight plugged in.

11 Keep the heat high. When the cooker reaches full pressure (first whistle), turn off the heat.

12 Open the cooker after the pressure subsides.

TO SERVE

1. Fluff up the pulao with a fork and spoon into a serving dish.
2. Garnish with mint leaves.
3. Serve hot.

You can use cauliflower florets instead of broccoli.

Serve with amla raita *(p. 168).*

A cup of cooked broken wheat provides over 5 grams of protein. When combined with the protein from the green peas and broccoli, it makes a protein-rich vegan/vegetarian meal.

CALORIES (KCAL)	PROTEIN	FATS	CARBOHYDRATES	FIBRE
304.5	8.7	4.5	58.9	3.3

(per serving)

Broken Wheat and Mixed-Sprout Khichdi with Fried Garlic

On nippy Bengaluru evenings, I'd happily settle for a bowl of steaming hot khichdi for dinner. A little shimmering puddle of ghee melting into the bowl of khichdi makes me feel as though all is well with the world.

Khichdi is a versatile dish. Add your choice of grain, dal, spices and veggies (or not) and you have a healthy, one-pressure-cooker meal ready in no time. This recipe mixes dalia or lapsi with mixed sprouted beans. The fried onions and garlic make it extra special.

SERVES 3

- 1 cup broken wheat (lapsi or dalia)
- 1 cup mixed sprouts (moong, moth beans or matki, horse gram or kulthi)
- 2 bay leaves
- ¼ tsp turmeric powder
- ½ tsp salt

THE TEMPERING

- 1 tbsp ghee
- 1 tsp cumin seeds (jeera)
- A pinch of asafoetida powder (hing)
- 1 medium-sized onion, finely sliced
- 8 cloves garlic, finely sliced

TO SERVE

- 1 tbsp ghee

1 Place the broken wheat in a bowl and wash it a couple of times.

2 Drain and add the sprouts.

3 Cover with fresh water and keep aside for 20 minutes.

4 Boil 4 cups of water in a 4-litre pressure cooker.

5 Add the broken wheat and sprouts to the boiling water with the bay leaves, turmeric powder and salt.

6 Close the pressure cooker with the lid and the pressure weight plugged in.

7 Cook the broken wheat and sprouts for 4–5 minutes over low heat after the cooker reaches full pressure (first whistle).

8 Open the cooker after the pressure subsides.

THE TEMPERING

1 Heat the ghee in a small frying pan.

2 Add the remaining tempering ingredients.

3 Fry over moderate heat for 7–8 minutes, till the onion and garlic turn golden-brown.

4 Pour the contents of the pan over the khichdi and mix well.

TO SERVE

1 Spoon the khichdi into 3 bowls.

2 Serve immediately while it is piping hot, with a tsp of ghee over each serving.

3 Fresh yogurt and a mango pickle make worthy accompaniments. Roasted papad is a bonus.

Choose sprouts made from smaller beans such as moong, moth and horse gram so they all cook uniformly.

Adding a cup of seasonal vegetables to the khichdi makes it even more nutritious and a one-pot balanced meal in its truest sense.

Given that most vegetarian food items are incomplete proteins (not containing all the essential amino acids), combining a grain with a pulse in a single dish provides both their amino acids, making it a complete protein source.

CALORIES (KCAL)	PROTEIN	FATS	CARBOHYDRATES	FIBRE
304.4	8.0	4.7	58.3	2.2

(per serving)

Sindhi Flatbread (Koki)

While preparing for my Class 12 exams, I attended Agrawal Coaching classes in Dadar (Mumbai). My benchmate was a girl who travelled all the way from Ulhasnagar, a suburb some 50 km away. She left home at 5 a.m. each morning, carrying with her a lunch box filled with divine Sindhi food. Come lunch break, the most arresting aroma would waft out of her box. It was from her lunch box that I first tasted *koki*. Even though it's been 25 years since then, every time I make this dish I am taken back to that cramped classroom and the hunger-inducing aromas emanating from that lunch box.

MAKES 10-12 pieces

THE DOUGH

- 1 cup wholewheat flour
- 1 cup sorghum flour (jowar)
- 1 tsp salt
- 2 tbsp ghee
- 2 tsp dried pomegranate seeds (anar dana)
- 1 tsp cumin seeds (jeera)
- 1 large onion, finely chopped
- 2 green chillies, finely chopped or ½ tsp red chilli powder
- 2-3 tbsp finely chopped fresh coriander leaves

TO COOK THE *KOKI*

- 2 tbsp groundnut oil

THE DOUGH

1 Mix the flours with the salt and ghee in a large bowl.

2 Lightly toast the pomegranate seeds and cumin seeds in a pan over moderate heat, till fragrant.

3 Cool and crush coarsely using a mortar and pestle.

4 Add to the flour mix along with the remaining dough ingredients.

5 Start kneading the dough using the moisture released from the onions.

6 Add water, a little at a time, while kneading to get a stiff dough.

7 Divide into 10–12 portions.

THE *KOKI*

1 Place a tava over moderate heat.

2 Roll out each portion of dough into a circle, slightly thicker than a paratha – around ¼-inch thick.

3 Place a *koki* on the tava and cook over moderate heat on both sides, pressing down with a sturdy spatula till golden spots appear.

4 Apply a few drops of oil on both sides and cook for 2 minutes per side.

5 The cooked *koki* will be golden, crispy and rather flaky.

6 Keep the cooked *kokis* wrapped in a clean kitchen towel or in an insulated case while you prepare the rest of them.

TO SERVE

1 Serve hot with yogurt for breakfast or as a snack along with tea.

Koki *is traditionally made using wholewheat flour. You can add coarsely-ground black pepper and ajwain to the koki, although anar dana is the key spice in this preparation.*

The high fibre, protein and iron content of sorghum (jowar) flour makes it a good candidate for replacing the flours in any recipe. It is also naturally gluten-free.

CALORIES (KCAL)	PROTEIN	FATS	CARBOHYDRATES	FIBRE
100.9	2.2	3.1	16.5	2.1

(per koki*)*

Roasted Root Veggies with Peanut-Tamarind Dip

Roasting brings out complex flavours from root vegetables such as carrots, beetroots, sweet potatoes and potatoes. The outsides turn golden-brown and crisp while the insides cook to a soft texture. The peanut-tamarind dip is my spin-off on a satay sauce. A tray of roasted veggies with the dip makes a unique appetizer to pass around at a party.

SERVES 4

1 large sweet potato
2 large carrots
1 large potato
1 large beetroot
2 tbsp olive oil
¾ tsp coarse salt

THE DIP
Please refer to p. 198

1 Preheat the oven to 190°C.

2 Line a baking tray with parchment paper. You may need to use two trays depending on the size of your oven.

3 Wash and scrub the vegetables and peel finely or simply scrub the surface till clean.

4 Slice the vegetables into ½-inch thick slices.

5 Keep the beetroot slices separate.

6 Toss the remaining vegetable slices in the olive oil and salt, reserving a little for the beetroot.

7 Toss the beetroot slices separately so that all the vegetables are not coloured pink.

8 Arrange the vegetable slices on the baking tray in a single layer, taking care not to overcrowd them. (Overcrowding the tray will result in the veggies steaming and not roasting.)

9 Put the tray in the centre of the preheated oven and roast for 20 minutes at 190°C, till the edges are golden-brown and a toothpick passes through the slices easily.

TO SERVE

1 Arrange the roasted veggies on a platter with the bowl containing the dipping sauce in the centre.

2 Serve with the dip on pg 146.

Lightly steaming chunks of root vegetables before roasting them cuts down the oven time. Make sure you pat the veggies dry before tossing them in oil.

No oven? Don't worry. Roast them over low heat in a heavy cast iron pan for 30 minutes or so, turning them around once in between.

Instead of root vegetables roast chunks of pumpkin, zucchini and onions and toss them as a salad with some cooked pasta.

Root vegetables, while being calorie-dense, are a good source of complex carbs and a nutritious replacement for grains. They also keep you feeling full for long. Most of them are rich in vitamins A and C, potassium and dietary fibre.

CALORIES (KCAL)	PROTEIN	FATS	CARBOHYDRATES	FIBRE
239.5	4.9	10.4	33.1	5.1

(per serving)

12: Steamed Millet Logs (*Muthiya*) with Fresh Greens

13: Overnight Savoury Millet Crêpes

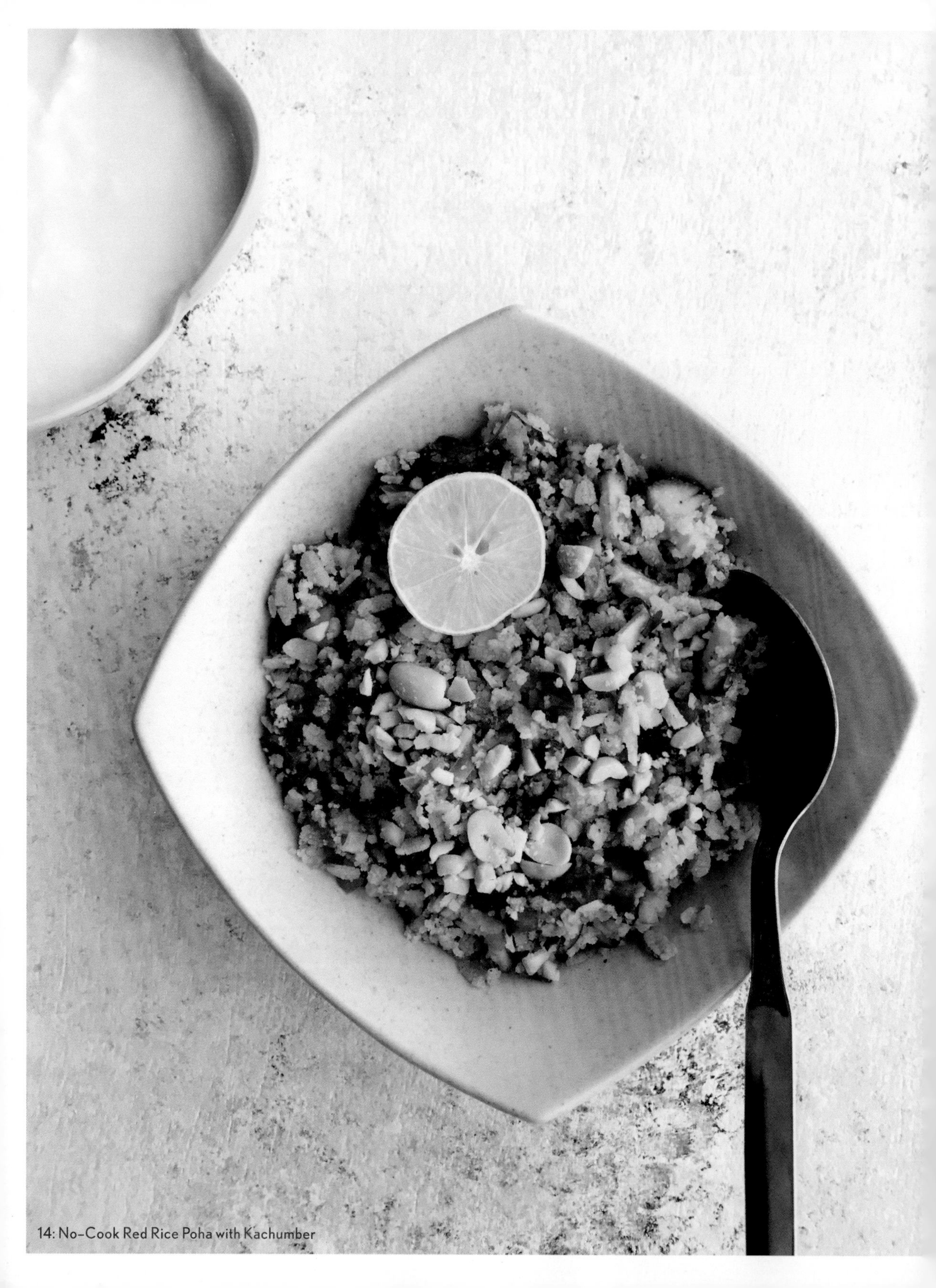

14: No-Cook Red Rice Poha with Kachumber

15: Savoury Waffles with Cucumber Chutney

16: Millet Fenugreek Salad

17: Purple Cabbage with Leafy Greens (*Thoran*)

18: Green Rice–Flour Dumplings

19: The Ultimate Superfood Burger

20: Roasted Carrot Soup with Basil Oil

21: Green Pancakes (Chile)

Gourmet Popcorn: Sweet and Savoury

If I know my 8-year-old son well, his two all-time favourite foods are popcorn and pancakes. I love to surprise him with different flavours of popcorn, both sweet and savoury. When I was testing out recipes for this book he was my self-appointed popcorn flavour approver. 'Mummy, first get the two-flavour combinations right, then you can work on three-flavour combinations,' encouraged my little gourmand. These two variations got the double-thumbs-up from him.

MAKES 3 cups each of sweet and savoury popcorn

THE COFFEE CARAMEL POPCORN

2 tsp peanut oil
1/3 cup dried corn kernels
1 tsp instant coffee powder
1/3 cup grated jaggery
¼ tsp cinnamon powder
½ tsp salt

THE MINT AND GARLIC-BUTTER POPCORN

1 tbsp salted butter
2 tsp olive oil
1/3 cup dried corn kernels
¼ tsp salt
1 tsp dried mint powder
¼ tsp turmeric powder
½ tsp garlic powder

THE POPCORN

1 Use dried corn kernels for these recipes and not the ready bags of microwave popcorn.

2 To pop the corn, use ⅓ cup of kernels per batch.

3 Heat the peanut oil or olive oil in a deep pan with a lid or in a large pressure cooker.

4 Add the corn, kernels and stir over high heat.

5 Once the first corn pops cover with a lid. If your pan has a handle shake the covered pan slightly periodically.

6 When the popping sounds stop you know that most of the corn has popped.

7 Remove the lid and stir over low heat for 1 minute or so, allowing all the dampness caused by the steam to dry out.

8 If you have a large enough pan pop the entire batch of corn and divide into two for the two flavours.

THE COFFEE CARAMEL POPCORN

1 Bring 2 tbsp of water to a boil in a small pan.

2 Reduce the heat to low and stir in the instant coffee.

3 Add the jaggery and cinnamon. Stir till the jaggery has melted.

4 Allow this to simmer over low heat for 6–7 minutes till the bubbles settle and the caramel is somewhat thick.

5 Pour this over one batch of popped corn and using two forks or spatulas make sure all the popcorn is coated with the caramel.

6 Sprinkle a pinch of salt over the popcorn and allow to cool completely before serving.

THE MINT AND GARLIC-BUTTER POPCORN

1 Melt the salted butter in a small pan over low heat.

2 Add the remaining ingredients, stir and remove from heat.

3 Allow the butter to get infused with the flavours for 5 minutes.

4 Pour this over the second batch of popcorn and toss well to combine.

More sweet flavours: coconut-jaggery; peanut-caramel. More savoury flavours: tomato powder-chilli; Italian herbs, olive oil and garlic.

Changing the base fat can also give you different flavours. For example, ghee, olive oil, coconut oil and mustard oil can be interchanged.

Store-bought microwavable bags of popcorn are full of hydrogenated fats or weird oil blends that mimic the taste of butter. Homemade popcorn is naturally gluten free and whole grain. You can also control the fat and sodium that goes into the popcorn. It also makes a very good snack option for diabetics.

CALORIES (KCAL)	PROTEIN	FATS	CARBOHYDRATES	FIBRE
209.2	3.0	7.9	32.9	3.4

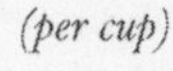

(per cup)

Savoury Waffles with Cucumber Chutney

Savoury waffles can be prepared with a mind-boggling variety of flours and flavours. They can be prettier versions of the traditional Indian pancakes. The inspiration for this recipe comes from the Andhra *pesarattu* which is made with a moong bean batter. The cucumber chutney makes these waffles so much more fun to eat.

MAKES

4 large waffles

THE WAFFLES

- ½ cup moong beans, soaked for 4 hours
- 1 cup quick-cooking oats
- 2/3 cup sorghum flour (jowar)
- 2–3 green chillies, roughly chopped
- 1 tsp salt
- ½ tsp baking soda
- 1 tsp baking powder
- 2 tbsp oil

THE CUCUMBER CHUTNEY

- 2 medium-sized cucumbers
- 1 packed cup fresh coriander leaves
- 2 green chillies, roughly chopped
- 4 tbsp yogurt

THE WAFFLES

1 Preheat a waffle iron or the oven (if you are using waffle moulds) at 220°C.

2 Blend all the waffle ingredients with 1 cup of water till you get a smooth, pourable batter.

IF USING A WAFFLE IRON

1 Brush the surfaces of the preheated waffle iron with oil. Spoon in the batter.

2 Close the lid and cook till the indicator light changes colour or the waffles are golden-brown.

IF USING WAFFLE MOULDS

1 Place silicone waffle moulds on a baking tray and pour the batter into the moulds till they are filled.

2 Put the tray in the centre of the oven preheated at 220°C and bake for 15 minutes until they are cooked through.

3 Remove the tray from the oven.

4 Invert the waffle moulds over the baking tray, gently peeling the moulds off.

5 Bake the reverse side for 5–6 minutes.

1 lemon, juiced
3 tbsp roasted gram (or roasted peanuts)
¾ tsp salt

THE CUCUMBER CHUTNEY

1 Peel the cucumbers and cut them in half lengthwise. Remove and discard the seeds. Dice the cucumber flesh.

2 Put the cucumber along with the remaining chutney ingredients in a small mixer jar.

3 Blend to make a smooth chutney.

4 Transfer to a small serving bowl.

TO SERVE

1 Serve the waffles with the green cucumber chutney for a hearty breakfast or a light lunch.

See photograph 15 of colour insert.

You can also serve them with a salad on the side.

If you plan to make these for breakfast remember to soak the moong beans overnight so that you can prepare the batter instantly.

If you don't have a waffle iron/mould, divide the batter into four portions and prepare pancakes. Serve them with the chutney.

For those who are gluten sensitive this makes a hearty gluten-free breakfast. Replace the yogurt in the chutney with soya or peanut yogurt and you can make it vegan too. A combination of oats, green moong and sorghum adds healthy fibre to your breakfast plate.

CALORIES (KCAL)	PROTEIN	FATS	CARBOHYDRATES	FIBRE
218.3	8.6	5.4	34.2	4.9

(per waffle)

Tomato Garlic Crackers

Homemade crackers are the best party appetizers you can make in advance. They also make a healthy snack to carry on board flights or on road trips. There's no limit to the number of variations you can have with this recipe simply by changing the flours and the flavour additions. Topping them with poppy or white sesame seeds adds another layer of crunch to these irresistible munchies.

SERVES

6 as appetizers

THE DOUGH

1 tsp active dry yeast
½ tsp sugar
1 cup wholewheat flour
½ cup corn meal
½ cup sorghum flour (jowar)
1½ tsp salt
1 tsp garlic powder
1 tsp red chilli powder
2 tbsp oil
2 tbsp tomato paste

TO ROLL

2 tbsp all-purpose flour

THE FLAVOURED OIL

1 tbsp oil
½ tsp paprika
1 tsp mixed dried herbs of choice
A pinch of salt

THE DOUGH

1 Mix the active dry yeast, sugar and ½ cup slightly warm water in a small bowl. Keep covered for 10 minutes, till the yeast turns frothy.

2 Mix all the dry ingredients for the dough in a large bowl.

3 Rub in the oil and tomato paste till uniformly incorporated.

4 Add the yeast and knead adding 1–2 tbsp of water if needed.

5 Continue kneading for 5–7 minutes and shape into a round ball.

6 Lightly oil the bowl and place the dough back in it.

7 Cover with a towel and keep in a warm place till it doubles in volume. This should take 1–2 hours.

TO ROLL

1 Knead the dough again and divide it into 6 portions.

2 Roll each portion with a slight dusting of flour into a tortilla/circle of ⅛-inch thickness.

3 Poke the crackers all over with the tines of a fork.

4 Place a skillet over low heat and partially cook both sides of the rolled out dough.

5 Remove and cut into desired shapes using a pizza cutter.

TO FLAVOUR

1 Mix the oil, paprika and dried herbs in a large bowl.

2 Toss the tortilla pieces in the flavoured oil.

TO BAKE

1 Preheat the oven to 180°C.

2 Arrange the pieces in a single layer on a baking tray lined with parchment paper. Sprinkle some salt over them.

3 Put the tray in the centre of the preheated oven and bake for 8 minutes.

4 Remove and keep aside to cool.

5 The crackers will get crisper on cooling.

TO SERVE

1 Serve with any dip of your choice or store them in an airtight container.

Instead of tomato paste and the other flavourings in this recipe you can add 1–2 tbsp of tomato pickle with the oil before kneading the dough.

CALORIES (KCAL)	PROTEIN	FATS	CARBOHYDRATES	FIBRE
196.2	4.7	5.7	32.5	4.1

(per serving)

Barley Soup with Pistou

The intensely flavourful pistou elevates this grain-based soup to another level of deliciousness. Hearty enough for a light meal, it spells comfort on a rainy day or a cold evening.

SERVES 4

THE SOUP

- ½ cup barley (jau), soaked for more than 2 hours
- 1 tbsp olive oil
- 1 tbsp finely chopped garlic
- 1 small onion, finely chopped
- 1 small carrot, finely chopped
- 1 celery stalk, finely diced
- ¼ tsp stock cube, crushed
- A few fresh basil leaves, finely chopped

THE PISTOU

- 1 packed cup Italian basil leaves
- 6 cloves garlic, roughly chopped
- 1 green chilli, roughly chopped
- Scant ½ tsp salt
- ½ a lemon, juiced
- 1 tbsp extra-virgin olive oil
- 1 medium-sized tomato

THE SOUP

1 Drain the barley grains and rinse well. Keep aside.

2 Heat the olive oil in a pressure cooker.

3 Fry the garlic, onion, carrot and celery for 1–2 minutes over moderate to high heat.

4 Add the drained barley grains, stock cube, basil leaves and 3½ cups of water, giving it a good stir.

5 Close the pressure cooker with the lid and the pressure weight plugged in.

6 Cook over high heat for two whistles.

7 Reduce the heat to minimum and cook for 8–10 minutes.

8 Open the cooker after the pressure subsides.

THE PISTOU

1 Blend all the ingredients for the pistou, except the tomato, in small mixer.

2 When done, transfer to a small bowl.

3 Cut the tomato into four quarters. Remove and discard the seeds.

4 Grate the tomato flesh, discarding the skin.

5 Whisk the tomato pulp into the prepared basil paste to mix well.

TO SERVE

½ tsp salt

½ tsp freshly ground black pepper

TO SERVE

1. Reheat the soup till boiling hot.
2. Season with salt and pepper.
3. Divide the soup between 4 soup bowls.
4. Top with a dollop of pistou and serve hot.

See photograph 7 of colour insert.

You can toss cooked pasta along with sautéed mushrooms into the prepared pistou for a quick weeknight dinner.

Pearl barley is a healthy whole grain rich in protein, fibre, selenium and manganese. Regular consumption of barley reduces LDL (bad cholesterol) and improves bowel function.

CALORIES (KCAL)	PROTEIN	FATS	CARBOHYDRATES	FIBRE
146.1	3.6	3.9	22.8	5.4

(per bowl)

Oat Flour and Potato Savoury Pancakes (Thalipeeth)

Thalipeeth is a popular Maharashtrian snack made with multigrain flour. The aromas from the roasted grains and spices make this a one-of-a-kind savoury pancake usually served with freshly churned white butter. My recipe is a simpler take on this traditional one, making use of oats and potatoes instead of a mix of flours. Serve for breakfast or as a teatime snack.

SERVES
6 *thalipeeths*

THE DOUGH
- 1 cup quick-cooking oats
- 2 tbsp + 2 tbsp roasted peanuts, divided
- 2 medium-sized potatoes, boiled
- 2–3 green chillies, finely chopped
- 1 tsp cumin seeds (jeera), lightly toasted
- 2–3 tbsp finely chopped fresh coriander leaves
- ¾ tsp salt
- 3 tbsp yogurt

TO COOK THE *THALIPEETH*
- 2 tbsp groundnut oil

THE DOUGH

1 Toast the oats in a frying pan over moderate heat for 3–4 minutes, till aromatic. Remove and keep aside to cool.

2 Grind the toasted oats in a mixer jar to get a coarse flour.

3 Add 2 tbsp of roasted peanuts and pulse for a few seconds.

4 Transfer to a large bowl.

5 Coarsely pound the remaining peanuts and add to the bowl.

6 Peel the potatoes and grate them into the bowl.

7 Mix in the green chillies, cumin seeds, coriander leaves and salt.

8 Add the yogurt a little at a time to bind the ingredients into a smooth dough. It should be fairly stiff.

THE *THALIPEETH*

1 Divide the dough into 6 portions and roll into balls.

2 Place a plastic sheet on the counter. Grease it with few drops of oil.

3 Place each ball of dough on the sheet and press out into a circle of ¼” thick and roughly 4” in diameter. Poke a hole in the centre.

4 Put a non-stick tava over moderate heat and lightly brush it with oil.

5 Place a *thalipeeth* on the tava and cook over moderate heat, adding a few drops of oil in the centre.

6 Press down with a spatula all around till the side being cooked is golden-brown. This will take 3–4 minutes.

7 Turn it over and cook similarly with a few drops of oil for another 3–4 minutes.

7 Cook the remaining *thalipeeth* in the same way.

TO SERVE

1 Serve hot with any chutney of your choice and a bowl of yogurt or a dollop of white butter.

Instead of oat flour you can use millet or sorghum flour to prepare the thalipeeth. *Toasting the flours gives a better flavour to the dish.*

Any leftover cooked rice or millets can also be kneaded along with oat flour and boiled potatoes to make the dough.

CALORIES (KCAL)	PROTEIN	FATS	CARBOHYDRATES	FIBRE
180.7	5.0	8.9	20.7	1.8

(*per* thalipeeth)

No-Cook Red Rice Poha with Kachumber

If I have to pick a favourite breakfast, it would be *kanda poha*, the Maharashtrian-style poha made with lots of onions, green chillies and the addition of potatoes or green peas. But in the summer, even the thought of standing in front of the hob and sautéing onions is tiresome. This is my go-to summer poha recipe. Think of it as a poha salad of sorts. Red-rice poha is more nutritious than white poha, and using the finer variety means that there is absolutely no need to cook or steam it.

SERVES 2

1 cup fine red rice poha

THE KACHUMBER

- 1 European cucumber (see notes on p. 53)
- 1 medium-sized onion
- 1 medium-sized tomato
- 3–4 tbsp fresh coriander leaves, finely chopped
- 1 lemon, juiced
- ½ tsp salt
- ¼ tsp red chilli powder

THE GARNISH

- 2 tbsp roasted peanuts

TO SERVE

- Lemon wedges

Wash the poha a couple of times and keep aside to drain through a sieve for 5–10 minutes.

THE KACHUMBER

1. Peel the cucumber and dice finely.
2. Finely chop the onion and tomato.
3. Mix the vegetables with the remaining kachumber ingredients in a bowl.

TO SERVE

1. Add the drained poha to the kachumber and toss well.
2. Divide between two bowls.
3. Coarsely pound the peanuts using a mortar and pestle, and sprinkle over the bowls of poha.
4. Serve with extra lemon wedges.

See photograph 14 of colour insert.

If you do want to dress this up a bit more, a tadka of mustard seeds, cumin seeds, green chillies and curry leaves in groundnut oil is a great idea. A few broken cashews added to the tadka and fried till golden-brown add more fun to this breakfast bowl.

Red-rice poha, made from unpolished red rice, is a better option for diabetics due to the higher fibre content in the bran. Comparing red rice with white rice, the former has a much stronger antioxidant value – almost over 10 times that of white and brown rice.

CALORIES (KCAL)	PROTEIN	FATS	CARBOHYDRATES	FIBRE
303.2	9.2	7.5	52.3	3.8

(per serving)

Millet Fenugreek Salad

Bye-bye, quinoa and kale! Hello, millet and methi (fenugreek). I love the surprise on my students' faces when I combine Indian greens and grains in my salad workshops. You can make a salad with whatever you have on hand. There's no need to go hunting for fancy or expensive ingredients, and this millet methi salad proves it. It stays good for a few hours after mixing, so feel free to pack this in lunch boxes too.

SERVES 3–4

THE SALAD

- 1 large carrot
- 1½ cups cooked foxtail millet (kangni)
- 1 cup cooked chickpeas (kabuli chana)
- ¾ cup tender fenugreek leaves (methi), without stems
- ½ cup fresh pomegranate arils

THE DRESSING

- 2 tbsp extra-virgin olive oil
- 2 tsp white wine vinegar
- ½ tsp panch phoron powder (Bengal five-spice powder; see cooking notes)
- ½ tsp freshly ground black pepper
- ½ tsp salt
- 1 tbsp honey

THE SALAD

1 Scrub the carrot and peel it.

2 Grate the carrot coarsely using a box grater.

3 Mix the grated carrot with the remaining salad ingredients in a large bowl.

THE DRESSING

1 In a small bowl whisk together all the dressing ingredients till thick and creamy.

TO COMPETE THE DISH

1 Pour the dressing over the salad and toss well to combine.

2 The millet and chickpeas absorb the flavours better if you refrigerate it for an hour.

Ensure that both the millet and chickpeas are cooked through but not mushy. Fluff up the millet grains as soon as they are cooked and refrigerate in an airtight container, till ready to use. See general cooking notes on how to cook millets (p. xxvi).

Use tender fenugreek leaves for this salad. Avoid the stems and tougher leaves.

To prepare panch phoron powder, lightly toast a tsp of panch phoron (see p. 6) over low heat. Once cooled, grind to a coarse powder. You can also use mustard powder or grainy mustard paste instead of panch phoron powder.

See photograph 16 of colour insert.

Use any kind of local greens you can find for the salad. Choose tender, smaller leaves for salads and use the tougher, more mature leaves in dishes like dal.

Studies have shown that polyphenols like tannins and anthocyanins in pomegranates have potential antioxidant, anti-inflammatory and anti-cancer effects. The antioxidant potential of pomegranate juice is more than that of red wine and green tea.

GARDENING TIP:

Soak fenugreek seeds in water for 34 hours. Drain and allow to sprout over 2 days in a jar. In a shallow tray of compost enriched loose soil, sprinkle the sprouts in a single layer. Spray water daily. In 8–10 days you will have a tray full of fenugreek micro greens that you can use in salads.

CALORIES (KCAL)	PROTEIN	FATS	CARBOHYDRATES	FIBRE
220.2	5.9	8.8	30.4	5.0

(per serving)

Overnight Oats with Sautéed Apples

With all the goodness of a bowl of oats with the comforting flavours of an apple pie, I can never say no to oats in this form. Overnight oats have a much better texture as compared to cooked oats in my opinion. Do remember to prep for this the previous night.

SERVES 1

THE OVERNIGHT OATS

½ cup instant oats (approx. 40 g)
1 tsp yogurt
¾–1 cup water or milk

THE SAUTÉED APPLE

1 medium-sized apple
1–2 tsp ghee

THE TOPPINGS

¼ tsp powdered green cardamom
2 tsp walnut bits, toasted

THE OVERNIGHT OATS

1. In a serving bowl, mix the oats with the yogurt and water or milk.
2. Cover with a lid and leave it on the counter top overnight.
3. You can also mix this in a glass jar with a lid.

THE SAUTÉED APPLE

1. Scrub and wash the apple well.
2. Cut the apple into half and slice finely, discarding the core and seeds.
3. Heat ghee in a cast iron or heavy-bottomed pan.
4. Layer the apple slices and cook over low heat for 10–12 minutes, till golden.
5. Shake the pan and allow to cook for 5 more minutes.
6. Add a spoon of water to dislodge any caramelized bits from the bottom of the pan. Remove from heat.

TO SERVE

1. Make a well in the centre of the oats.
2. Add the caramelized apples and top with the cardamom powder and toasted walnuts.

See photograph 22 of colour insert.

You can use extra toppings such as desiccated coconut, honey and a dollop of yogurt to make it even more irresistible.

The contents of the bowl can be blended with 2 ice cubes to make a delicious breakfast smoothie.

Replace oats with cooked millets, brown rice or poha. Allow to set overnight and make your own breakfast bowl by topping with fruits and nuts.

A combination of oats, apples and walnuts makes this porridge a fibre-rich breakfast. As apple skin has plenty of nutrient-rich flavonoids and polyphenols, try and use organic apples so that you don't need to peel them.

CALORIES (KCAL)	PROTEIN	FATS	CARBOHYDRATES	FIBRE
364.0	9.9	15.5	46.5	7.9

(per serving)

Brown Rice and Horse Gram Sprout Salad

Horse gram is a pulse used in several traditional cuisines of India. Called *kollu* in Tamil, *ulavalu* in Telugu, *kulith* in Marathi and *kulthi* in Hindi, horse gram is also popular in Kumaoni and Garhwali dishes. Horse gram sprouts add a boost of protein, calcium and iron to dishes. This not-so-popular pulse needs to be brought back into vogue because of its high nutritive value.

SERVES 3–4

THE SALAD

- 1 medium-sized mango, raw or semi-ripe
- 2 cups cooked brown rice
- 1 cup horse gram (kulthi) sprouts
- ½ cup fresh pomegranate seeds
- 2–3 tbsp finely chopped fresh coriander leaves
- ½ tsp salt
- ½ tsp freshly ground black pepper

THE TEMPERING

- 2 tbsp coconut oil
- A pinch of asafoetida powder (hing)
- ½ tsp mustard seeds
- 1 tsp cumin seeds (jeera)
- 2 sprigs fresh curry leaves
- 2–3 green chillies, finely sliced
- 1 tbsp lemon juice

THE SALAD

1. Peel the mango and dice it.
2. Combine the mango along with the remaining salad ingredients, except the seasonings, in a large bowl.
3. Season with salt and pepper and toss well.

THE TEMPERING

1. Heat the coconut oil in a small pan.
2. Temper the asafoetida powder, mustard seeds and cumin seeds.
3. When the seeds splutter, add the curry leaves and green chillies.
4. Give it a stir and remove from heat.
5. Add the lemon juice and mix well.

TO SERVE

1. Pour the contents of the pan over the salad ingredients.
2. Garnish with fresh coconut and serve.

Use ripe or raw mango as per the season.

THE GARNISH

2–3 tbsp grated fresh coconut

In the absence of brown rice, use cooked short- or long-grain white rice for this salad.

For tips on cooking brown rice, see p. xxvi.

The other ingredients in the salad such as the sprouts, coconut, coconut oil, etc. bring down the glycaemic index of the dish, causing a slower rise in blood glucose. This makes a good lunch box salad for diabetics.

Sprouting horse gram reduces the level of anti-nutrients – phytates and oxalic acid – and thus improves the absorption of antioxidants and minerals such as calcium, iron and copper.

CALORIES (KCAL)	PROTEIN	FATS	CARBOHYDRATES	FIBRE
188.0	4.1	6.1	29.9	3.1

(per serving)

My Glorious Panzanella Salad

Panzanella is a simple rustic salad from Tuscany comprising stale bread and tomatoes. My version is heartier, and glamorous enough to take centre stage on a brunch table. Make sure to load up a bit of everything in one forkful for maximum enjoyment.

SERVES 2–4

THE SALAD

- 2 cups cherry tomatoes or 3 medium-sized tomatoes
- 2 tsp olive oil
- 1–2 sprigs fresh rosemary
- 3 thick slices of a sourdough loaf (approx. 100 g)
- 2 European cucumbers (see notes on p. 53)
- A small handful of fresh mint leaves
- 2 cups fresh lettuce leaves
- 4 eggs, hard-boiled
- ½ tsp freshly ground black pepper

THE DRESSING

- 3 tbsp extra-virgin olive oil
- 3 tbsp lemon juice
- ½ tsp salt
- A pinch of turmeric powder

THE SALAD

1 Halve the cherry tomatoes.

2 If using regular tomatoes, cut into quarters and then into bite-sized chunks.

3 Heat the oil in a medium-sized frying pan.

4 Throw whole sprigs of rosemary into the hot oil to infuse the oil with its flavours.

5 Add the tomatoes and allow to brown over high heat, tossing lightly off and on. The tomatoes will soften slightly. Don't let them collapse into a mush. This will take around 3–4 minutes.

6 Spread them out in a dish and keep aside.

7 Tear the sourdough bread into bite-sized pieces and toss them in the same pan over moderate heat for 3–4 minutes, till lightly toasted.

8 Remove and keep aside.

9 Slice the cucumber lengthwise and then into thick slices on the diagonal.

10 Keep the mint leaves in a small bowl of cold water.

TO ASSEMBLE

1 Tear the lettuce leaves into bite-sized pieces and make a bed on a salad platter.

2 Scatter the bread chunks over this.

3 Top with the cucumbers.

4 Arrange the browned tomatoes around the platter.

5 Drain the mint leaves, pat dry and strew them over the salad.

6 Peel the eggs and slice them lengthwise in half.

7 Arrange the pieces around the dish.

8 Top with coarsely ground black pepper.

THE DRESSING

1 Put all the ingredients for the dressing in a small jar.

2 Close the jar and shake it till the dressing is thick and creamy.

TO SERVE

1 Drizzle the golden dressing all over the salad, reserving a couple of tsp to top while serving.

2 Refrigerate for 1 hour before serving.

If you prefer, use soft boiled eggs with the bread soaking up the oozing yolks.

Feel free to add finely sliced onions, red radishes and any other salad-friendly vegetables to this panzanella.

Cooked tomatoes are rich in lycopene which, while having all the usual health benefits of a powerful antioxidant, also improves fertility levels in men. They have also been proved to decrease the incidence of strokes and prostate cancer in men.

CALORIES (KCAL)	PROTEIN	FATS	CARBOHYDRATES	FIBRE
270.7	10.6	17.3	19.0	2.5

(per serving)

Stuffed Plantain Kebab

This recipe makes a quick batch of appetizers for your Indian menu-themed party. An ordinary-looking kebab from the outside, a hot and sweet surprise awaits you when you take a bite. You can easily scale up the recipe to make a larger batch.

SERVES
6 kebabs

THE KEBAB MIX
- 1 large plantain or cooking banana (approx. 350 g)
- ¼ tsp garlic powder or 1 garlic clove, grated
- ½ tsp salt
- ½ tsp cumin powder (jeera)
- ½ tsp coriander powder
- 2 tbsp finely chopped fresh coriander leaves
- A pinch of red chilli powder

THE STUFFING
- 8–10 seedless raisins
- 3 dried apricots
- 2 green chillies
- 2 tsp grated fresh coconut
- 1 tsp chaat masala powder
- 2 tbsp finely chopped fresh coriander leaves

TO COOK THE KEBABS
- 2 tbsp oil

THE KEBAB MIX

1 Place the whole, unpeeled plantain in a 2 litre+ pressure cooker with ½ cup of water.

2 Close the pressure cooker with the lid and the pressure weight plugged in.

3 Put it over high heat and remove after 2 whistles.

4 Open the cooker after the pressure subsides.

5 Remove the plantain, and peel it when cool enough to handle.

6 Put the plantain in a large bowl and mash it.

7 Add the remaining ingredients for the kebabs and mix well.

8 Divide into 6 portions. Keep aside.

THE STUFFING

1 Finely chop the raisins, apricots and green chillies.

2 Transfer to a bowl with the rest of the stuffing ingredients.

3 Mix well and divide into 6 portions.

TO SHAPE THE KEBABS

1 Shape the 6 portions of the kebab mix into small cups.

2 Place a portion of the stuffing in the hollow of each cup.

3 Bring the ends of the kebab mix together, seal and shape into patties.

TO COOK THE KEBABS

1 Heat the oil in a non-stick frying pan over moderate heat.

2 Shallow-fry the kebabs for 6–8 minutes on each side, till golden-brown and crisp.

TO SERVE

1 Serve hot with any chutney of your choice or with tomato ketchup.

Try this recipe with potatoes or sweet potatoes. The kebab mix can be shaped into smaller koftas. Shallow fry or bake them and add to a curry base to make a kofta curry.

Cooking bananas or plantains are rich in resistant starch. These are carbs that resist digestion, reaching the large intestine intact and acting as a prebiotic for the good bacteria in the gut.

CALORIES (KCAL)	PROTEIN	FATS	CARBOHYDRATES	FIBRE
93.7	0.8	4.4	14.0	1.7

(per serving)

Banana and Buckwheat Pancakes

Pancakes are always in demand in my home. My son is the pancake connoisseur and that by default means that we adults also indulge in this breakfast every once in a while. The term 'indulge' is a bit of a misnomer here. These banana and buckwheat pancakes, while neatly taking care of two overripe bananas, also use no refined flour or sugar, making it one of my favourite recipes. The buckwheat flour gives these pancakes a darker colour and a nuttier flavour with a slightly grainy texture. Serve them with a good maple syrup and all will be forgiven!

MAKES
6 pancakes

THE PANCAKE BATTER
- ½ cup buckwheat flour (kutu)
- ½ cup wholewheat flour (atta) or multigrain flour
- 1 tsp baking powder
- ½ tsp baking soda
- 1 tsp cinnamon powder
- 2 overripe medium-sized bananas
- 2 eggs
- 1 tbsp oil
- 1/3 cup milk

TO COOK THE PANCAKES
Oil as required

TO SERVE
Maple syrup or honey

THE PANCAKE BATTER

1 Sift all the dry ingredients for the batter into a bowl and mix well.

2 Peel the bananas and place in a medium-sized bowl.

3 Mash the bananas coarsely using the tines of a fork.

4 Add the eggs and whisk well.

5 Mix in the oil and milk. Whisk to combine.

6 Make a well in the centre of the dry ingredients.

7 Pour in the banana mix and stir, till there are no lumps and the batter is smooth.

8 At this point the bowl can be covered with cling film and refrigerated for 1–2 hours. Or you can prepare the pancakes immediately.

TO COOK THE PANCAKES

1 Heat or place a non-stick frying pan over moderate heat.

2 Using kitchen paper smear the surface of the pan with ½ tsp oil.

3 Once the pan is moderately hot, ladle the batter (roughly ¼ cup) into the pan.

4 Allow it to spread out naturally. You may nudge the batter into a proper round if that is something you prefer.

5 Cook over moderate heat. The pancake will puff up and almost double in height as bubbles appear around the circumference.

6 Using a spatula, flip the pancake over and cook the other side for 45 seconds to a minute.

7 Remove on to a plate and keep warm.

8 Make the remaining pancakes in the same way.

TO SERVE

1 Stack 3 pancakes each on 2 plates.

2 Pour some pure maple syrup or honey over the pancakes for added sweetness.

See photograph 8 of colour insert.

You can make two pancakes, around 4" in diameter, in a reasonably large-sized pan. You can also try using the same batter to prepare banana buckwheat muffins. Add some chopped walnuts or frozen blueberries and a sprinkling of coconut on the top for a perfectly healthy portable breakfast. Seal the bag of buckwheat flour and keep refrigerated so it does not spoil.

Buckwheat has a unique composition of amino acids that helps lower bad cholesterol and high blood pressure and improves digestion. It is rich in fibre and naturally gluten free. One cup of buckwheat flour provides around 15 grams of protein and 12 grams of fibre.

CALORIES (KCAL)	PROTEIN	FATS	CARBOHYDRATES	FIBRE
134.0	4.5	4.6	19.8	2.2

(per pancake)

Little Millet Tomato 'Rice'

At any given time I have at least three kinds of millets in my pantry. It is so easy to make almost any dish healthier by substituting the processed carbohydrate with this humble wholegrain. Ever since I spotted them in a farmer's market six years ago in Bengaluru, I have been sold on their goodness. Tomato rice is a popular rice variety in Tamil homes. Substituting millet for polished white rice improves the nutritional quotient of this dish considerably.

SERVES 3

1 cup little millet (kutki)
5–6 medium-sized tomatoes
1 tsp salt

THE TEMPERING

1 tbsp sesame oil (gingelly oil)
A pinch of asafoetida powder (hing)
½ tsp mustard seeds
¼ tsp fenugreek seeds
1 tbsp husked, split Bengal gram (chana dal)
2–3 tbsp raw peanuts
2–3 dried red chillies
2 sprigs fresh curry leaves
½ tsp turmeric powder
½ tsp red chilli powder

1 Wash the millets in several changes of water. Drain and keep aside.

2 Chop the tomatoes and keep aside.

THE TEMPERING

1 Heat the oil in a 4-litre pressure cooker. Stir in the asafoetida powder.

2 Add the mustard seeds.

3 When they splutter, stir in the fenugreek seeds, dal, peanuts and red chillies.

4 Stir on moderate to high heat till the chana dal and peanuts crisp up.

5 Strip the curry leaves from the stalk and drop them into the oil. The leaves will crackle to a crisp.

6 At this point, stir in the turmeric powder and chilli powder.

TO COMPLETE

1 Add the chopped tomatoes with the salt. Stir over high heat for 4–5 minutes, till the tomatoes are almost pulpy.

2 Transfer the washed and drained millets into the pressure cooker and fry for 2–3 minutes along with the other ingredients.

3 Pour in 2 cups of water and bring to a boil over high heat.

4 Close the pressure cooker with the lid and the pressure weight plugged in.

5 Turn off the heat when the cooker reaches full pressure (first whistle). The millets will continue cooking in the residual steam in the cooker.

6 Open the cooker after the pressure subsides.

7 Stir through, separating the grains. Remove and store in a casserole which will keep the dish warm.

Don't let the cooked millets sit in the pressure pan or any utensil you cook it in. It will dry out and turn lumpy. Fluffing it up and transferring to a casserole will keep the grains separate.

Serve it as is for breakfast or with a cup of raita for a light lunch.

CALORIES (KCAL)	PROTEIN	FATS	CARBOHYDRATES	FIBRE
174.4	4.3	4.9	28.9	5.4

(per serving)

Steamed Millet Logs (Muthiya) with Fresh Greens

My first memories of *muthiya* are from when I stayed overnight at my friend Surbhi's house. We were studying together to tackle the mammoth subject, Medicine, for our final MBBS exams. Surabhi's mother kept plying us with delicious food at regular intervals. I remember her running the grain mill at home, grinding chana dal into to a fine flour and preparing *muthiyas* with it. The aroma and flavour of this snack is something I can never forget. Here is my adaptation of the famous Gujarati snack. (This recipe needs a steamer.)

SERVES 4 as a snack

THE DOUGH

- 1/3 cup gram flour (besan)
- 1/3 cup maize meal (makkai atta)
- 1/3 cup sorghum flour (jowar)
- 1 cup grated bottle gourd
- 1 small carrot, grated
- ½ cup finely chopped tender spring onion greens
- ¼ cup finely chopped fresh coriander leaves
- 1 tsp grated fresh ginger
- 3 green chillies, finely chopped (optional)
- 1 tbsp white sesame seeds
- ¼ tsp baking soda
- 1 lemon, juiced
- 1 tbsp yogurt
- ½ tsp salt

THE DOUGH

1 Combine all the ingredients for the dough in a large bowl.

2 Using your fingers, bring the ingredients together to form a soft dough.

3 The bottle gourd and carrot will release their juices. This, along with the moisture from the lemon juice and yogurt, provides enough liquid to make a dough.

4 Divide into 3 portions.

TO STEAM THE *MUTHIYAS*

1 Set up a steamer by filling a large pan with 3 inches of water. Grease the steamer basket with a few drops of oil and place it over the pan. Cover with a lid and bring the water to a boil.

2 Shape the 3 portions of dough into logs, a little over 1" in diameter. If it sticks to your fingers, dip your hands in water before shaping them.

3 Place the logs carefully into the steamer basket, leaving some space between them.

4 Cover and steam cook for 10–12 minutes.

THE TEMPERING

1 tbsp oil

2 tsp white sesame seeds

1 tsp mustard seeds

2–3 sprigs fresh curry leaves

5 Remove and allow to cool completely.

6 At this point, the logs can be refrigerated and the *muthiyas* given their final toss in oil just before serving, or you can proceed with the tempering.

7 Slice the steamed logs into ½"–¾" thick slices and arrange them on a serving platter.

THE TEMPERING

1 Heat the oil in a small pan.

2 Add the sesame and mustard seeds.

3 When they stop spluttering, strip the curry leaves off their stems and add. Fry till crisp.

4 Pour the contents of the pan over the hot *muthiyas.*

5 The other option is to transfer the sliced *muthiyas* into the tempering and shallow fry them, till crisp and golden.

TO SERVE

1 Serve hot with any green chutney of your choice.

See photograph 12 of colour insert.

Shallow-fried muthiyas *make an excellent travel snack.*

Use any leftover vegetable pieces, grate them and add to the dough. If you don't have a steamer, the same dough can be thinned down further and used to prepare bite-sized, thick pancakes.

CALORIES (KCAL)	PROTEIN	FATS	CARBOHYDRATES	FIBRE
151.2	3.9	5.8	21.7	4.1

(per serving)

Green Rice-Flour Dumplings

Some dishes, specific to certain festivals, get their outing just once a year. They are even prefixed with the festival name – in this case, *nonbu adai*. On this festival, two kinds of *adai* are made – savoury and sweet. This recipe is my take on the savoury *adai*, incorporating fresh herbs such as curry leaves and coriander leaves that not only add a pleasant green colour to the dish but also give it a refreshing herbaceous flavour. Two-bite-sized steamed rice flour dumplings with a touch of green goddess – you'll love this traditional recipe with a twist.

MAKES 20 *adais*

THE DOUGH

- 1 cup rice flour
- 2 handfuls of fresh coriander leaves, roughly chopped
- 4 sprigs fresh curry leaves, stripped and roughly chopped
- 1" piece fresh ginger, roughly chopped
- 2–3 green chillies, roughly chopped
- ¼ cup grated fresh coconut
- ¾ tsp salt
- 2 tbsp desiccated coconut bits (copra; optional)

THE TEMPERING

- 1 tsp oil
- 2 sprigs fresh curry leaves

THE DOUGH

1 Toast the rice flour in a heavy-bottomed pan over moderate heat for 7–8 minutes, till aromatic.

2 In a 3-litre pan, bring 1¾ cups of water to a boil.

3 Grind the coriander leaves, curry leaves, ginger, green chillies and fresh coconut to a coarse paste using 1–2 tbsp water.

4 Add this paste to the boiling water along with the salt.

5 Once the water returns to a boil, add the toasted rice flour to the water. Turn off the heat.

6 Cover with a lid and keep aside for 5 minutes.

7 Open the pan and use a spatula to incorporate the flour into the water and make a smooth dough.

8 Return the pan to low heat and keep mixing continuously, till there are no lumps of flour and you have a soft dough.

9 Remove the dough on to a plate to cool.

THE CHUTNEY (*TULSI THOGAYAL*)

- 1 tsp oil
- 1 tbsp husked, split black gram (urad dal)
- ½ tsp mustard seeds
- 2 small flakes of tamarind
- 3 dried red chillies
- ½ cup grated fresh coconut
- 1 packed cup fresh tulsi leaves (holy basil)
- ¼ tsp salt

THE GARNISH

- 1 tsp oil
- 1 sprig of fresh curry leaves

THE CHUTNEY

1 Heat the oil in a small pan.

2 Fry the dal in the hot oil, till golden.

3 Add the mustard seeds, tamarind and red chillies and fry for 1 more minute.

4 Remove from the heat and transfer the contents to a mixer jar when cool.

5 Add the coconut, basil leaves and salt, and grind to make a coarse chutney. Transfer the chutney to a small bowl and keep aside.

TO PREPARE THE GARNISH

1 Heat the oil in the same pan and fry the curry leaves to a crisp.

2 Drain and set aside.

TO COOK THE DOUGH

1 Divide the cooled dough into 20 lemon-sized balls.

2 Flatten the balls slightly and poke a hole in the centre like a doughnut; tuck a bit of dried coconut in the hole.

3 Set up a steamer by filling a large pan with 3 inches of water. Grease the steamer basket with a few drops of oil and place it over the pan. Cover with a lid and bring the water to a boil.

4 Arrange as many dumplings as you can in the basket without overcrowding. Steam for 10 minutes.

TO SERVE

1 Remove and arrange the *adai* on a platter.

2 Fill the hole in the centre of the *adais* with the prepared chutney and top with some fried curry leaves. Serve hot with some more chutney on the side.

See photograph 18 and 33 of colour insert.

You can add some grated carrot to the boiling water along with the green paste. Regular coconut chutney or coriander mint chutney can be served as an accompaniment instead of the thogayal.

CALORIES (KCAL)	PROTEIN	FATS	CARBOHYDRATES	FIBRE
43.3	0.7	1.7	6.1	0.6

(*per* adai)

Overnight Savoury Millet Crêpes

On our trip to Amsterdam, a tiny eatery called Pancakes Amsterdam near the Anne Frank museum came highly recommended from a friend. When we arrived it was freezing cold and raining and they had a waiting period of more than 30 minutes. Still, we persisted, praying that the wait would be worth it. When we were seated, the variety of sweet and savoury crêpes on the menu made it difficult to choose. We went with one sweet, one savoury and one American-style for the kid, and everything was so good! The savoury crêpe with goat cheese, spinach, pine nuts and garlic oil is my inspiration for this recipe. Please note that overnight preparation is required for this recipe.

MAKES
4 thin 8-inch crêpes

THE CRÊPE BATTER
- 1/3 cup sorghum flour (jowar)
- 1/3 cup red rice flour
- 1/3 cup finger millet flour (ragi)
- 1 tsp raw cane sugar
- ¼ tsp active dry yeast

THE TOPPING
- 200 g paneer
- ½ cup fresh mint leaves
- ¼ cup grated fresh coconut
- ½ tsp red chilli flakes
- ½ tsp salt
- 1 lemon, juiced

TO COOK THE CRÊPES
- ½ tsp salt
- ¼ tsp oil

THE CRÊPE BATTER

1 Mix all the batter ingredients in a large bowl.

2 Add ¾ cup of water and use a wire whisk to mix, till smooth.

3 Cover and keep aside overnight or for 6–8 hours, till the mixture is frothy and has increased in volume.

4 At this point, you can mix in the salt and prepare the crêpes right away or cover and refrigerate for a few hours till you plan to prepare the dish. Remember to bring the batter to room temperature before using it.

THE TOPPING

1 Prepare the topping just before preparing the crêpes.

2 Grate the paneer coarsely into a flat dish.

3 Pluck out the mint leaves. Refresh in cold water, remove, pat dry and chop fine.

4 Add this to the paneer along with the coconut, chilli flakes, salt and lemon juice. Toss gently with your fingertips and keep aside.

TO COOK THE CRÊPES

1 Mix the salt into the batter.

2 Place a large non-stick frying pan over moderate heat.

3 Wipe the surface of the pan with a few drops of oil using a folded piece of kitchen paper.

4 Ladle a little over ½ a cup of batter on to the centre of the medium-hot pan and with quick concentric circles spread the batter from the centre outwards to make as thin a crêpe as possible.

5 This will cook very quickly, taking only about 30 seconds.

6 Turn over carefully and cook the other side if desired.

TO SERVE

1 Remove the crêpe on to a plate and sprinkle the topping over it.

2 Repeat with the other crêpes.

3 Serve hot.

See photograph 13 of colour insert.

Use any cheese instead of paneer. A smoked cheese adds tons of flavour.

A sweet topping using cream cheese, sliced banana, hazelnut chocolate sauce and coarsely chopped walnuts is equally delicious.

CALORIES (KCAL)	PROTEIN	FATS	CARBOHYDRATES	FIBRE
189.3	8.2	9.5	18.1	1.4

(per crêpe)

Herby Bamboo Rice Salad

A salad loaded with herbs, this recipe has bundles of flavour in every bite. My herby bamboo rice salad is inspired from the Middle Eastern *tabbouleh* that is a mix of couscous, parsley and mint, all drenched in a hearty douse of extra-virgin olive oil. Please note that bamboo rice needs soaking overnight and has a longish cooking process.

SERVES 4

- ½ cup bamboo rice (raw)
- 1 medium-sized onion
- 2 tbsp white vinegar
- 1 large tomato
- ½ cup finely chopped tender spring onion greens
- ½ cup finely chopped fresh coriander leaves
- 2 green chillies
- 1 tbsp lemon juice
- 1 tbsp extra-virgin olive oil
- 1 tsp salt
- 3 tbsp pumpkin seeds, salted

1 Wash the bamboo rice and soak it in a bowl of water overnight or for 6–8 hours. Drain the water.

2 Combine the rice with 1½ cups of water in a pan that fits into the pressure cooker. Place this in the cooker.

3 Close the pressure cooker with the lid and the pressure weight plugged in.

4 Put the cooker over high heat and allow 4 whistles.

5 Reduce the heat to minimum and cook for 20 minutes.

6 Open the cooker after the pressure subsides.

7 The cooked rice will have a bite to it. Chill the rice or bring it to room temperature before using it in the salad.

8 Peel the onion, cut it in half and finely slice. Soak it in a bowl containing 1 cup of water and 2 tbsp vinegar for 10 minutes, to take the bite off the raw onions.

9 Quarter the tomatoes and scoop out and discard the seeds. Finely dice the tomato flesh and keep aside.

10 Slit the green chillies vertically. Scrape out and discard the seeds using a small spoon. Finely chop the flesh and keep aside.

11 Remove the sliced onions from the water, squeeze well and place them in a large bowl. Add the cooked rice, prepared vegetables and remaining ingredients.

12 Toss well to combine.

13 Refrigerate for 2–3 hours and serve chilled.

See photograph 5 of colour insert.

Bamboo rice has a thick outer layer, thereby taking a long time to cook. Cook till the grain bursts open to ensure that it is soft enough to chew and digest. Cooking bamboo rice in a pan on a stovetop will take over an hour.

You will find bamboo rice in natural food stores.

Bamboo rice is obtained from bamboo in its flowering stage, mostly collected from forests. It is a good source of vitamin B6, fibre and protein.

CALORIES (KCAL)	PROTEIN	FATS	CARBOHYDRATES	FIBRE
122.1	4.3	4.4	16.7	8.0

(per serving)

Baked Tapioca Chips

Tapioca is a root vegetable much loved in Kerala where it is called *kappa*. Boiled tapioca is usually eaten with fish curry in these parts. These tapioca chips baked in the air fryer are so unbelievably crunchy that you will forget that they are not deep-fried. No air fryer? No problem! There are instructions for baking them in the oven too. You need a heavy-duty peeler for this one.

SERVES 2

- 1 large tapioca (yucca) (approx. 350–400 g)
- 2 tsp groundnut oil
- Salt, to taste

1. Pre-heat the air fryer or oven at 190°C.
2. Wash and scrub the muddy exterior of the tapioca.
3. Using a sturdy peeler, peel the outer brown skin and discard.
4. Using the same peeler, continue peeling through the length of the tapioca, going all around the circumference to get thin strips.
5. Pat the tapioca strips dry using thick kitchen paper.
6. Toss the strips in a large bowl with the oil and a pinch of salt.

IF USING AN OVEN

1. Layer the tapioca strips on a baking tray lined with parchment paper or a silicon mat.
2. Put the tray in the centre of the oven preheated at 190°C and bake for 8–10 minutes, till you see the edges turn golden.

IF USING AN AIR FRYER

1. Put the tapioca strips into the basket.
2. Open the basket and toss well every 2 minutes.
3. The tapioca chips should be crisp in around 6 minutes.

TO SERVE

1 Remove the chips to a serving bowl and sprinkle a pinch of salt over them.

2 Serve immediately with hummus or any other dip of your choice.

See photograph 3 of colour insert.

Other vegetables and fruits that you can bake into similar chips are plantain, carrot, beetroot, sweet potato, okra (bhindi, cut into juliennes), aubergine (baingan), apple, pear and potato.

Serve with Bengal gram hummus (p. 152).

Tapioca is a very calorie-dense root, rich in calcium and fibre. It is one of the healthier options to include in the diet for people who are desirous of gaining some weight.

CALORIES (KCAL)	PROTEIN	FATS	CARBOHYDRATES	FIBRE
248.3	1.1	2.3	56.1	1.4

(per serving)

Meal in a Bowl: Buckwheat Noodles in Broth

A noodle bowl like this spells comfort, with health and taste in each spoonful. Put this down in your menu plan for a weeknight dinner and it won't disappoint. This bowl tastes good both hot and cold.

SERVES 2

THE BROTH

4 spring onions, only the white part
1 small onion, quartered
1 small carrot, scrubbed and roughly chopped
3–4 lemon grass blades, roughly chopped
1" piece fresh ginger, sliced
3 cloves garlic, smashed with peel
A large handful of fresh coriander stalks
3"–4" celery stalk, roughly chopped
½ tsp salt

THE NOODLES

100 g buckwheat noodles (soba)

THE VEGETABLES

2 tsp oil
1 tsp white sesame seeds
1 bok choy, roughly chopped

THE BROTH

1 Combine all the ingredients for the broth in a medium-sized pan with 3½ cups of water. (Do note that you don't need to peel or finely chop any of the vegetables and aromatics that go into the making the broth.)

2 Put the pan over high heat and bring to a rolling boil.

3 Reduce the heat, cover the pan and simmer for 15–20 minutes.

4 Pour the contents of the pan through a sieve into a fresh pan. Press down on the solids in the sieve to extract all the flavour.

5 Discard the solids.

THE NOODLES

1 Fill a large pan halfway with water and bring to a boil over high heat.

2 Drop the soba noodles into the boiling water, and cook for 5–6 minutes, or as indicated on the pack.

3 As soon as the noodles are cooked, drain and soak in a bowl of cold water.

THE VEGETABLES

1 Put the oil in the same pan over high heat.

2 Stir in the sesame seeds along with the prepped vegetables.

½ medium-sized onion, sliced
4–5 brussels sprouts, quartered

THE GARNISH
1 egg, hard-boiled or soft-boiled
½ tsp black sesame seeds
Fresh red chillies, very finely sliced
Tender spring onion greens, very finely sliced
Round red radish, very finely sliced

3 Stir-fry over high heat till the vegetables are slightly charred.

TO ASSEMBLE

1 Pour 1 cup of broth into each of the 2 soup bowls.

2 Drain the noodles from the cold water using a pair of tongs and divide them between the bowls.

3 Top with the stir-fried vegetables and half an egg, hard-boiled or soft-boiled, as per your choice.

4 Sprinkle black sesame seeds over the egg.

5 Garnish with the red chillies, spring onion greens and red radish.

6 Don't forget to keep both chopsticks and a soup spoon handy.

See photograph 10 of colour insert.

If you can't find buckwheat noodles use plain egg noodles.

Instead of bok choy and brussels sprouts, feel free to use any vegetables you have on hand.

To make this dish vegan, use stir-fried or baked tofu instead of egg.

Prepare extra broth and use as a stock for soups.

Buckwheat has a unique composition of amino acids that helps lower bad cholesterol and high blood pressure, and improves digestion.

CALORIES (KCAL)	PROTEIN	FATS	CARBOHYDRATES	FIBRE
209.1	9.9	8.3	20.7	2.5

(per serving)

Flavour-Bursting Corn Bread

If you are new to baking, this is one recipe that will have you beaming at the results. The corn bread turns out flawlessly moist, despite minimal oil. You'll find bursts of distinct flavours in every bite – the briny black olives, tart sun-dried tomatoes, sweet corn kernels and shards of heat from the jalapeño bits. This is also potluck-friendly!

MAKES

1 loaf (approx. 8" x 4")

THE DRY INGREDIENTS

- 1 cup maize meal (makkai atta)
- ½ cup wholewheat flour
- 1 tsp baking powder
- ½ tsp baking soda
- 1 tsp salt
- 2 tsp raw cane sugar

THE WET INGREDIENTS

- 1 cup buttermilk
- ¼ cup milk
- 1 egg (for eggless version, see cooking notes)
- 2 tbsp oil + some more for brushing the tin

THE ADDITIONS

- 1 tbsp sun-dried tomatoes, soaked in warm water for 10 minutes
- 2 tbsp finely chopped fresh oregano or 1 tsp dried oregamo

1 Preheat the oven at 180°C.

2 Brush a loaf tin (8½"x 4½" or roughly 1 litre in volume) with oil, taking care to coat the corners well.

3 Mix the dry ingredients in a large bowl using a wire whisk.

4 Whisk all the wet ingredients in a medium-sized bowl.

5 Make a well in the centre of the dry ingredients and tip in the wet mixture.

6 Use a spatula or spoon to combine the dry and wet ingredients till no lumps remain.

7 Drain the soaked sun-dried tomatoes and stir them into the batter along with the oregano, jalapeño bits and corn kernels.

8 Scrape the dough into the prepared loaf tin.

9 Stud the surface of the batter with black olive slices.

10 Put the tray in the centre of the oven and bake at 180°C for 40 minutes, till a skewer inserted into the centre of the loaf comes out clean.

11 Cool in the pan for 5 minutes.

1 tbsp finely chopped jalapeño
pickled 2 tbsp corn kernels, fresh or frozen
2 tsp black olives, sliced

11 Loosen the corn bread from the edges using a knife and turn it over a cooling rack. Cool for 15–20 minutes before slicing.

12 Serve with a Mexican salad or a bean stew.

See photograph 11 of colour insert.

Buttermilk is the liquid left over after removing freshly churned butter. 1 cup milk + 1 tsp vinegar allowed to sit for 5 minutes can be used instead of buttermilk.

For an eggless version, combine 1 tbsp flaxseed meal with 2 tbsp boiling hot water. Whisk well till frothy. Keep aside for 5 minutes and then use instead of the egg in the recipe.

The same dough can be baked in an 8" or 9" square baking tin. In such a case, baking time will be reduced to 20–25 minutes.

CALORIES (KCAL)	PROTEIN	FATS	CARBOHYDRATES	FIBRE
58.9	1.6	2.5	7.8	0.8

(per loaf)

22: Overnight Oats with Sautéed Apples

23: Green Apple Rasam

24: Summer Yogurt Soup (Dahi ka Shorba)

25: Rainbow Salad with Citrus and Olive Oil Dressing

26: Mango Arugula Salad

27: Roasted Aubergine and Labneh on Pita

28: Avocado, Coconut Chips and Whole Bengal Gram Salad

29: Black-Eyed Pea Burgers

30: Petha Curry

protein punch

'What do you eat for protein?' If you a vegetarian (or a vegan), I'm sure you've heard this question all your adult life. People do realize the importance of protein as an essential ingredient for good health, but can't understand how to incorporate it in a vegetarian diet.

Protein is vital for the development of new tissues and overall growth during our childhood. In adulthood, protein helps in regeneration of tissues and a whole host of biochemical processes that sustain life itself. During pregnancy and lactation, sufficient protein intake is essential for the growth of the foetus and for the production of breast milk.

Presence of eight essential amino acids is required in any food to call it a complete protein. Proteins from cereals, legumes and vegetables are considered to be of a poorer quality than animal protein because of poorer digestibility and absorption, and also because they are usually lacking in one or more essential amino acids. Combining cereal with a legume, as is very common in Indian cuisine, however, makes the dish a complete protein as this combination provides all the essential amino acids. Combining cereal with legumes and dairy makes it an even more unbeatable protein source for vegetarians. For example: Dal khichdi with yogurt. Protein-rich snacks such as portioned-out nuts, cheese, a roasted lentils mix or homemade nut-and-grain bars make the best portable small meals for adults as well as kids. This also ensures that the protein requirement for the whole day is met.

As per guidelines*, protein intake for an Indian adult should be around 1g/kg body weight. The requirement is higher in children between 1–4 years and for pre-adolescents.

Beans, lentils, whole grain breads, soya products, dairy products, nuts and nut butters, eggs, vegetables, cereals (rice, wheat, oats, quinoa, etc.) all contribute towards the protein requirement for lacto-ovo-vegetarians.

In this section, you'll find soups, salads and appetizers made using a variety of lentils and beans. Mixed lentils mini adai, baked egg cups and green moong pancakes will give you ideas to start your day with a protein boost.

*Nutrient requirements and recommended dietary allowances for Indians as per a report by the Indian Council of Medical Research 2009.

Chickpea Za'atar Croquettes

The world has woken up to the nutritional worthiness of the humble Kabuli chana. This a vegetarian's go-to ingredient for extra protein, fibre, calcium and more. Chickpeas add heft to salads, soups, appetizers and mains. These croquettes make good two-bite-sized appetizers. Stuff them into a pita pocket with a crunchy salad and some hot sauce, and you have a portable lunch ready.

SERVES
8 croquettes

THE CROQUETTE MIX
- 2 cups cooked chickpeas (kabuli chana), drained
- ½ cup cooked unpolished rice
- 2 tbsp *za'atar*
- ½ tsp sumac
- ¼ tsp salt

TO COOK THE CROQUETTES
- 2 tbsp olive oil

THE CROQUETTE MIX

1 Put all the ingredients for the croquette mix in a large bowl.

2 Using a potato masher, mash everything to make a smooth paste.

3 Divide into 8 portions.

4 Shape into rounds or thick fingers and place on a dish or baking tray.

5 Cover with cling wrap and refrigerate for a minimum of 2 hours.

TO COOK THE CROQUETTES

1 Place a skillet or tava over moderate heat. Smear with 1–2 tsp of olive oil.

2 Cook the croquettes 4 at a time, roughly 8–10 minutes per side, till golden and crisp, using a few drops of olive oil around each piece.

3 Serve with labneh (p. 20) or inside a pita sandwich.

See photograph 31 of colour insert.

Za'atar is a fragrant Middle Eastern spice mix made with dried herbs, sesame seeds and salt. You can use a mix of dried oregano and thyme, along with white sesame seeds instead of za'atar. The same dough can be shaped into balls, deep-fried (or air fried), till golden-brown and crisp to make falafels.

Protein and fibre-rich chickpeas in a meal keep you full for longer. Combining chickpeas with rice in this recipe makes it a source of complete protein, providing all the essential amino acids.

CALORIES (KCAL)	PROTEIN	FATS	CARBOHYDRATES	FIBRE
88.7	3.7	2.6	12.5	2.9

(per croquette)

Jordanian Lentil Soup (Shourbat Adas)

On my trip to Jordan in 2016, our visit to the ancient city of Petra started with a Jordanian cooking workshop at a local restaurant. Among other dishes, we learnt to make this traditional lentil soup. A bowl of hot soup with fresh-from-the-oven pita bread was a treat for lunch. With a few tweaks, this has become one of my favourite soup recipes.

SERVES 4

½ cup masoor dal
3–3½ cups vegetable stock or water
2 tbsp olive oil
½ tsp coarsely crushed cumin seeds (jeera)
1 small onion, finely chopped
1 garlic clove, finely minced
½ tsp salt
½ tsp freshly ground black pepper
⅛ cup finely chopped curly parsley

THE GARNISH

½ tsp coarsely crushed cumin seeds
⅛ cup finely chopped curly parsley
½ tsp sumac
2 tsp extra-virgin olive oil

1 Wash the dal and soak it in a bowl of water for 1 hour.

2 Bring the vegetable stock or water to a boil in a pan over high heat.

3 Drain the soaked dal and add it to the pan.

4 Lower the heat and simmer for 25–30 minutes, till the dal is well cooked. Remove any scum that floats on the surface during this process.

5 Pass the cooked dal through a chinois or a fine meshed strainer, pressing down on it with a wooden ladle.

6 Heat the olive oil in a large frying pan. Stir in the cumin seeds, onion and garlic. Fry over moderate heat for around 5–6 minutes until the onion softens.

7 Pour in the mashed dal.

8 Season with salt and pepper and simmer for 2 minutes.

9 Stir in the parsley.

10 Divide the soup between 4 soup bowls.

11 Garnish each with a sprinkle of cumin, parsley, sumac and ½ tsp of extra-virgin olive oil.

12 Serve hot with toasted pita bread halves.

¼ cup tomato puree can be added to the soup during the final simmering stage.

This soup makes for a light dinner when paired with bread. Add fattoush, tabbouleh and hummus and you have a hearty Jordanian spread.

Soluble fibre in lentils reduces the levels of bad cholesterol (LDL), thereby preventing heart disease. The dietary fibre in lentils also slows down post-meal blood sugar spikes, making it a healthy addition to diabetic diets. While lentils have a significant portion of carbohydrates, a large percentage of it is resistant starch that does not impact blood sugar levels as much as refined grains.

CALORIES (KCAL)	PROTEIN	FATS	CARBOHYDRATES	FIBRE
169.5	7.5	5.1	19.2	3.9

(per serving)

Double Beans with Greens

When double beans are in season you will find these shelled beans, with a beautiful pink and white speckled colour being sold in the markets. At other times of the year, you can use dried beans which are speckled maroon and white. Soak in water overnight and proceed with the same recipe.

SERVES 2

200 g fresh double beans
1 tbsp olive oil
2 tbsp finely chopped garlic
1 medium-sized onion, finely sliced
2 cups shredded greens of choice (spinach, amaranth, radish greens)
4 tbsp tomato paste
1 tsp dried, mixed herbs of choice
½ tsp smoked paprika
½ tsp red chilli powder
¾ tsp salt

1 Wash the beans, drain and keep aside.

2 Put the oil in a medium-sized pressure cooker over moderate heat.

3 Fry the garlic for a few seconds.

4 Add the onion and fry for 1–2 minutes over low heat.

5 Add the greens and stir for a minute, till they wilt.

6 Stir in the tomato paste, herbs and spices.

7 Add the salt, 1 cup of water and the double beans.

8 Close the pressure cooker with the lid and the pressure weight plugged in.

9 Cook the beans for 5 minutes over low heat after the cooker reaches full pressure (first whistle).

10 Open the cooker after the pressure subsides.

11 Remove the stew into a bowl.

TO SERVE

1 Serve with sliced crusty bread or any cooked grains.

Simmer the stew over low heat for 5–6 minutes to thicken it. It makes an excellent sauce to top off a mound of cooked pasta. The beans and greens get pressure-cooked in the same time it takes the pasta to cook. You can put dinner on the table in under 15 minutes!

Allow garlic to rest for 15 minutes after chopping, slicing or grating before using it in cooking. This helps activate allicin, a compound linked to the cardiovascular, antibacterial and anti-cancer benefits that garlic is known for.

CALORIES (KCAL)	PROTEIN	FATS	CARBOHYDRATES	FIBRE
201.6	10.6	7.4	24.5	7.4

(per serving)

White Beans with Yogurt Dressing

This curd-rice inspired salad will truly amaze you. *Moar molaga*, the star ingredient here, are chillies marinated in sour yogurt and sundried. Usually made in traditional Tamil kitchens, *moar molaga* is easily available in most supermarkets these days.

SERVES 2–4

1 cup cooked white beans
1 medium-sized onion, finely chopped
1 medium-sized tomato, finely chopped
1 cup hung yogurt
½ tsp salt

THE TEMPERING

2 tbsp sesame oil (gingelly oil)
2–3 *moar molaga* (see cooking notes)
A pinch of asafoetida powder (hing), optional
1 tbsp chana dal
1 tbsp urad dal
1 tsp mustard seeds
½ tsp fennel seeds (saunf)
2 sprigs fresh curry leaves

THE GARNISH

2 tbsp fresh mint leaves, chopped

1 Combine the cooked beans, onion and tomato in a large bowl.

2 Place the hung yogurt in a medium-sized bowl and whisk well.

THE TEMPERING

1 Heat the oil in a small pan or a tempering ladle.

2 Add the *moar molaga* and fry, till it turns crisp.

3 Fish out the fried chillies using a slotted spoon and place on kitchen paper. Crush the chillies and keep aside.

4 Add the asafoetida powder and the dals to the same pan. Fry over moderate heat, till they turn light brown.

5 Add the mustard seeds. When they splutter, stir in the fennel seeds and curry leaves and fry for a few seconds.

THE DRESSING

1 Transfer the crushed chillies and tempering into the yogurt.

2 Season with salt and mix well.

3 Spoon this dressing over the beans and toss gently to combine.

TO SERVE

1 Garnish with fresh mint leaves and serve.

You will find moar molaga *packets in most supermarkets in the South and in South Indian dominated localities in other parts of India. If you don't find it, then go ahead and use plain dried red chillies.*

Make sure the beans are cooked through but not cooked to a mush.

To get 1 cup of hung yogurt, line a sieve with 2 layers of muslin cloth. Put in 2 cups of plain yogurt and allow to drain over a bowl in the refrigerator for 3–4 hours.

White beans or navy beans are rich in protein, 19 grams per cup and over 12 grams of fibre. The high fibre content has been shown to have a protective effect against colon cancer.

CALORIES (KCAL)	PROTEIN	FATS	CARBOHYDRATES	FIBRE
162.9	6.6	6.4	15.9	4.2

(per serving)

Mushrooms and Spring Onions in Chilli Garlic Sauce

This Indo-Chinese-style quick stir-fry is a weeknight dinner saviour. It takes less than 15 minutes to make from start to finish and there's no compromise on flavour. Keep a pot of noodles to boil while making this dish. Drain and toss in some hot sesame oil infused with garlic and white sesame seeds. You have a full meal on the table in under 20 minutes.

SERVES 2

200 g button mushrooms
4–5 spring onions
1 medium-sized onion
2 tsp finely chopped fresh ginger
1 tbsp finely chopped garlic
3–4 fresh green or red chillies, sliced
1 tbsp peanut oil
2 tsp cornflour
1 tbsp dark soya sauce
1 tsp white vinegar
2 tsp honey
A pinch of salt, if needed
Black pepper, freshly ground, to taste

1 Cut the mushrooms into halves or quarters, depending on their size.

2 Chop the tender green portion of the spring onions into 1" batons.

3 Slice the onion.

4 Keep the ginger, garlic and chillies handy as everything will need to go in quickly once the oil is hot.

5 Heat the oil in a large pan over high heat.

6 Add the aromatics, i.e. the spring onion greens, the sliced onion, ginger, garlic and chillies.

7 Give them a stir, add the mushrooms and toss well.

8 Stir-fry over high heat till the mushrooms turn golden-brown.

9 Prepare a slurry of corn flour, soya sauce, honey and vinegar in ¼ cup water.

10 Add this to the cooked mushrooms, stirring continuously, till the sauce acquires a nice sheen.

11 Season with a pinch of salt if required. Finish with freshly ground black pepper.

12 Serve hot with plain steamed rice, fried rice or simple garlic noodles.

Prepare a quick crisp salad of cabbage, cucumber and carrots tossed in vinegar, salt and chilli flakes and make a noodle bowl using some chilli garlic noodles, this mushroom stir-fry and an omelette (if you eat eggs). This hearty meal in a bowl is quick enough for a weeknight.

CALORIES (KCAL)	PROTEIN	FATS	CARBOHYDRATES	FIBRE
176.3	4.9	7.9	20.8	3.0

(per serving)

Green Pancakes (Chila)

Gram flour or other dal-based chilas may be a popular breakfast dish in parts of North India but for a lazy cook like me, chilas make an easy substitute for rotis. Inspired by the popularity of green goddess recipes all over the Internet, I have added a lively bunch of chopped greens to the batter, making it look vibrant and giving it a boost of nutrients.

SERVES 4–5 chilas

THE CHILA BATTER

1 cup gram flour (besan)
2 tbsp yogurt
½ tsp turmeric powder
1 tsp coriander powder
¼ tsp baking soda
1 tbsp lemon juice
1 tsp salt
2 cups finely chopped mixed greens (spring onions, bathua, spinach), etc. or bathua and spinach

TO COOK THE CHILAS

2 tbsp oil

THE CHILA BATTER

1 Combine all the ingredients for the chila batter in a large bowl.

2 Add 1 cup of water and mix well, till you get a smooth, light and pourable batter.

3 Cover and keep aside for 30 minutes.

TO COOK THE CHILAS

1 Place a non-stick tava over moderate heat.

2 Grease the tava uniformly with ¼ tsp oil using kitchen paper.

3 The tava should be fairly hot but not sizzling hot. Pour ½ cup of batter in the centre.

4 Using the back of the ladle, quickly spread the batter to cover the entire tava, roughly 8" in diameter.

5 Pour around ½ tsp oil around the chila and allow it to cook for 2–3 minutes, till golden and lightly crisp at the base.

6 Gently turn over and cook the other side for 1 minute or so.

7 Remove from the pan and place on a dish.

8 Prepare the remaining 3–4 chilas in a similar manner.

TO SERVE

1 Serve warm with any chutney of your choice or, for a heavier meal, serve them with a side dish such as a paneer bhurji or vegetable curry.

See photograph 21 of colour insert.

You can use any seasonal greens in this recipe, but remember to chop them really fine so that they cook in the same time that the chila cooks. Try substituting some of the gram flour with rice flour for a crisper texture.

Bengal gram or chana dal, from which besan is ground, has a very low glycaemic index. This means it has a negligible impact on increasing blood sugar post consumption, making it an excellent food choice for diabetics. Besan is also naturally gluten free and a good flour option for gluten-sensitive people.

CALORIES (KCAL)	PROTEIN	FATS	CARBOHYDRATES	FIBRE
86.4	3.8	3.6	9.8	2.0

(per chila)

Green Paneer Scramble (Bhurji)

Got some crumbly homemade paneer in the refrigerator? Look no further. Make this green paneer scramble. What makes this recipe special is that there is as much of green foliage in the dish as there is paneer, cranking up more points on the nutrition metre. Heap up some paneer bhurji on slices of whole-wheat bread for a wholesome, filling meal.

SERVES 2

200 g fresh paneer

THE TEMPERING

- 1 tbsp ghee or oil
- ½ tsp cumin seeds (jeera)
- ¼ tsp turmeric powder

THE OTHER INGREDIENTS

- 2 green chillies, sliced
- 1 medium-sized onion, finely chopped
- 1 small green bell pepper, finely chopped
- 3–4 spring onions, tender green portion, finely sliced
- 1 cup finely chopped mixed greens
- ¾ tsp salt
- 1 tsp coriander powder
- ½ tsp garam masala powder
- 2–3 tbsp finely chopped fresh coriander leaves

Crumble the paneer and keep aside.

THE TEMPERING

1 Heat the ghee or oil in a frying pan.

2 Add the cumin seeds.

3 When they start to splutter, stir in the turmeric powder.

TO COMPLETE

1 Add the green chillies, onion and bell pepper.

2 Fry over moderate heat for 4–5 minutes till the onion and bell pepper are nearly cooked.

3 Add the spring onion greens as well as the mixed green leaves. Stir over high heat till the greens are wilted but retain their vibrancy.

4 Tip in the crumbled paneer.

5 Season with salt.

6 Add the coriander powder, garam masala powder and coriander leaves. Stir well to combine all ingredients. Cover and cook for 1–2 minutes over low heat.

7 Remove into a bowl.

8 Serve hot with rotis, chila or toast.

Homemade paneer works well in this dish as you don't need neatly cut cubes.

Once the bhurji is ready, transfer into a bowl immediately and serve as the residual heat in the pan can make the paneer rubbery.

CALORIES (KCAL)	PROTEIN	FATS	CARBOHYDRATES	FIBRE
368.6	21.0	26.2	12.7	2.8

(per serving)

Oven-Roasted Crisp Dals

Deep-fried chana dal, masoor dal or moong dal tossed in salt and an addictive mix of spices is a popular snack. Salty and crisp, they make for a happy accompaniment at tea time. Deep-fried snacks with tea could do with a healthy replacement. Oven-roasted crisp dals are almost as good as the fried ones. Do note that this recipe needs some prep time for soaking and boiling the dals.

SERVES 4

1 cup whole masoor dal
2 tsp oil
½ tsp + ¼ tsp salt
1 tsp melted ghee
½ tsp red chilli powder
1 tsp chaat masala

1 Wash the dal and soak it in plenty of water for 4 hours.

2 Bring a medium-sized pan of water to boil.

3 Drain the soaked dal and add it to the boiling water. Boil for barely a minute and drain using a colander, shaking off all the excess water.

4 Spread the dal on an absorbent kitchen towel to soak up any moisture.

5 Meanwhile, preheat the oven to 190°C.

6 Line a baking tray with parchment paper or aluminium foil.

7 Transfer the dal from the kitchen towel to a medium-sized bowl.

8 Add the oil and ½ tsp salt and toss gently to coat well.

9 Tip the dal on to the lined baking tray, spreading it around.

10 Place the tray in the centre of the preheated oven and roast for 5 minutes.

11 Lower the temperature to 180°C and roast for 20 minutes till the dal turns golden-brown in colour. Take care not to burn the dal.

12 Remove from the oven and set aside to cool. It will get crisper as it cools.

13 Mix ¼ tsp of salt, the chaat masala powder, chilli powder and melted ghee in a small bowl.

14 Add this flavoured ghee to the crisp dal and mix well to coat evenly.

15 Once cool, stock in an airtight container.

You can prepare a larger batch of the dal, taking care not to overcrowd the baking tray.

The spices are added to the ghee and then used to coat the crispy baked dal so that they don't burn in the oven.

The same process can be used with husked, split Bengal gram (chana dal). The baking time will increase by 5–7 minutes.

Lentils have a considerable percentage of resistant starch, which enters the colon undigested, thereby not having much of an effect on blood sugar levels. The resistant starch acts as a prebiotic, helping promote growth of healthy bacteria in the colon, resulting in a healthy gut.

CALORIES (KCAL)	PROTEIN	FATS	CARBOHYDRATES	FIBRE
180.8	12.0	2.2	28.3	5.0

(per serving)

Sprouted Moong Chutney

Sprouted moong in a salad is the done thing. But how about using sprouts in a chutney? I love spreading this spicy chutney over crisp dosas for a masala dosa with a twist. Use fried gram if you don't have grated coconut handy.

MAKES
enough to spread over 4 dosas

¾ cup moong sprouts

THE TEMPERING
- 2 tsp coconut oil
- ½ tsp cumin seeds (jeera)
- ¼ tsp mustard seeds
- 1 tsp finely diced fresh ginger
- 5–6 fresh curry leaves

THE OTHER INGREDIENTS
- 1 small onion, chopped
- 1 green chilli, chopped
- 1 small tomato, chopped
- ¼ cup grated fresh coconut
- ½ tsp salt

1 Bring a small pan of water to boil with a pinch of salt over high heat.

2 Blanch the moong sprouts for 2–3 minutes in the boiling water. Drain immediately and keep aside.

THE TEMPERING

1 Heat the oil in a small frying pan.

2 Add the cumin seeds and mustard seeds.

3 When the seeds splutter, stir in the ginger and curry leaves and fry for 30 seconds.

TO COMPLETE

1 Mix in the onion, green chilli and tomato. Fry till the onion is translucent and the tomato is cooked to a pulp.

2 Transfer the contents of the pan into a mixer jar along with the blanched sprouts, fresh coconut and salt. Grind to a coarse paste.

TO SERVE

1 Make dosas and smear this chutney over them. Roll up and eat. No other accompaniments are needed.

Take care not to cook the sprouts to a mush to prevent the chutney turning too watery. You can also add a couple of cloves of garlic along with the ginger.

Stuff the dosa with a veggie or paneer mix to make it a hearty meal.

CALORIES (KCAL)	PROTEIN	FATS	CARBOHYDRATES	FIBRE
167.5	4.3	10.5	14.5	6.0

(per serving)

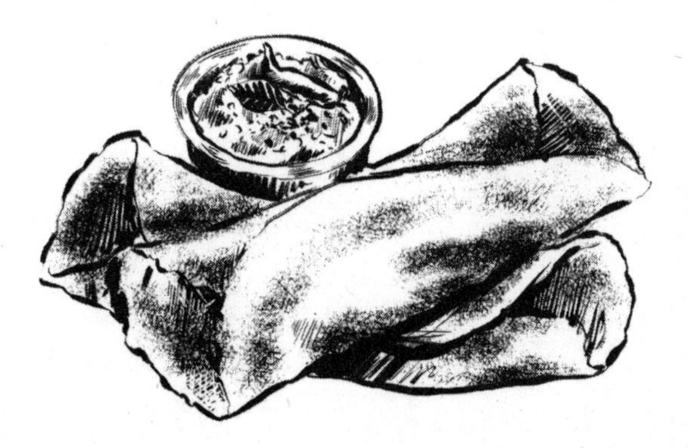

Black-Eyed Pea Burgers

In Indian cuisine, black-eyed peas or lobia are usually made into a spicy curry served with parathas or rice. However, these hearty beans can be used in a lot more dishes such as soups, salads and burgers. This burger recipe makes a good meatless option for vegetarians and vegans.

MAKES

2 burger patties

THE PATTY MIX

½ cup black-eyed peas (lobia), soaked overnight
2 small onions, finely chopped
1 tsp dried mixed herbs of choice
½ cup dry breadcrumbs (whole-wheat bread)
½ tsp salt
½ tsp black pepper, freshly ground
½ tsp fresh ginger, grated

TO COOK THE PATTIES

2 tbsp oil

THE PATTY MIX

1 Drain the black-eyed peas and rinse thoroughly.

2 Place them in a pressure cooker with 2 cups of water.

3 Close the pressure cooker with the lid and the pressure weight plugged in.

4 Cook the peas for 3–4 minutes over low heat after the cooker reaches full pressure (first whistle).

5 Open the cooker after the pressure subsides.

6 Drain the cooked beans through a sieve and transfer them to a bowl.

7 Add all remaining ingredients and mix well.

8 Mash the mixture well.

9 Divide into 2 portions and shape into burgers.

10 Keep them on a plate, cover with cling wrap and refrigerate for a minimum of 2 hours.

TO COOK THE PATTIES

1 Heat the oil in a frying pan.

2 Remove the patties from the refrigerator and shallow-fry them on both sides for approximately 7–8 minutes on each side till golden-brown.

TO SERVE

1 Serve with a salad or inside a burger bun with all the other trimmings of a burger.

See photograph 29 of colour insert.

Shape into small bite-sized kebabs and deep-fry or shallow-fry them to serve as appetizers.

CALORIES (KCAL)	PROTEIN	FATS	CARBOHYDRATES	FIBRE
361.3	11.8	15.6	43.9	4.5

(per patty)

Spicy Double Bean Mash

When you spot beautiful pink-and-white speckled beans in your local market don't walk past them. These seasonal fresh beans have a unique flavour and cook to a delightfully buttery texture. I cook double beans in quite a few ways and this hummus-inspired mash is one of them.

MAKES
1 cup of mash

THE CHILLI-GARLIC PASTE
2 dried red chillies
2 cloves garlic

THE BEANS
1 cup fresh double beans
½ tsp salt

THE TEMPERING
1 tbsp oil
A pinch of asafoetida powder (hing)
½ tsp cumin seeds

THE OTHER INGREDIENTS
1 small onion, halved and finely sliced
2–3 tbsp finely chopped fresh coriander leaves
½ a lemon, juiced
A pinch of salt

THE CHILLI-GARLIC PASTE

1 Soak the red chillies and garlic in a cup of hot water for 30 minutes.

2 Drain and grind them to a coarse paste.

3 Keep aside.

THE BEANS

1 Put the beans in a pressure cooker with 2 cups of water and ½ tsp salt.

2 Close the pressure cooker with the lid and the pressure weight plugged in.

3 Cook the peas for 2–3 minutes over low heat after the cooker reaches full pressure (first whistle).

4 Open the cooker after the pressure subsides.

5 Drain the beans and put them in a bowl. Mash with a fork and keep aside.

THE TEMPERING

1 Heat the oil in small frying pan.

2 Add the asafoetida powder and give it a quick stir.

3 Add the cumin seeds.

TO COMPLETE

1 When the seeds splutter, reduce the heat and add the onion.

2 Sauté over low heat for 8–10 minutes, till the onion is caramelized.

3 Add the chilli-garlic paste and stir-fry over high heat for 1 minute. (Keep the exhaust fan on or a window open when you do this, as frying the chilli paste can irritate your eyes and nose.)

4 Add the mashed beans, coriander leaves, lemon juice and a pinch of salt if required.

5 Stir well and remove into a small serving bowl.

6 Serve with tomato garlic crackers (p. 85).

Use this mash to top toast or spread over a dosa like a masala. It also makes a healthy dip to go with baked nachos.

If fresh double beans are not in season, use dried ones similarly after soaking overnight in water.

CALORIES (KCAL)	PROTEIN	FATS	CARBOHYDRATES	FIBRE
100.0	4.8	4.8	9.8	3.3

(per cup)

Spinach, Avocado and White Bean Dip

The goodness of beans and spinach, the creamy texture of avocado and the flavours of garlic and basil make this a dip you cannot resist double dipping into. Stock your fridge with a healthy dip like this to go with baked crackers or veggie sticks for those early evening snack cravings. Stir in a spoon of chilli oil if you like a spicy kick.

MAKES
1 generous cup of dip

- 2 cups spinach leaves
- ½ cup white beans, soaked in water overnight or 1 cup drained canned beans
- 1 ripe small avocado
- ½ a lemon, juiced
- 4 cloves garlic, roughly chopped
- A small handful of basil leaves
- ½ tsp salt
- ½ tsp freshly ground black pepper

THE SPINACH

1 Bring a pan of water to a boil over high heat.

2 Immerse the spinach leaves in boiling water for 2 minutes. Keep a bowl of iced water handy. Remove the wilted spinach with a pair of tongs and shock in iced water to stop the cooking and retain the bright green colour.

3 Drain the blanched spinach, gently squeezing out all the water.

THE BEANS (IF NOT USING CANNED BEANS)

1 Drain the beans and rinse well.

2 Put the beans in a pressure cooker with just enough water to cover and a pinch of salt.

3 Close the pressure cooker with the lid and the pressure weight plugged in.

4 Cook the beans for 6–7 minutes over low heat after the cooker reaches full pressure (first whistle).

5 Open the cooker after the pressure subsides.

6 Drain the beans and keep aside. Allow to cool to room temperature.

THE AVOCADO

1 Cut open the avocado and scoop out the flesh.

2 Squeeze lemon juice over the flesh to prevent from browning.

TO COMPLETE

1 Put the blanched spinach, cooked beans, avocado flesh, garlic and basil in a blender jar and season with salt and pepper.

2 Blend to make a smooth puree.

TO SERVE

1 Serve as a dip along with crudités or as a spread for a sandwich.

Unlike a traditional hummus, there is no extra olive oil added to the dish.

Here's another interesting dish to make with this dip: Skip the avocado and add as much whole-wheat flour as required, along with a pinch of salt, to the puree and knead to get a smooth dough. Make parathas using this dough.

CALORIES (KCAL)	PROTEIN	FATS	CARBOHYDRATES	FIBRE
247.0	10.3	18.5	13.0	8.3

(per cup)

Crispy Tofu Rice Paper Rolls

People love to hate tofu. But treat it right and you will look forward to eating this protein-rich food more often. Rice paper rolls are an easy no-cook dish that makes the most impressive appetizers with the least effort. Rolling them neatly takes a bit of practise, but once you get that right, there will be no stopping you!

MAKES 8 rolls

200 g firm tofu block

THE MARINADE

1 tsp grated fresh ginger
2 tbsp soya sauce
1 tbsp honey
1 tsp hot chilli sauce
2 tsp rice vinegar
¼ tsp freshly ground black pepper
1 tsp white sesame seeds
½ tsp sesame oil
1 large carrot

THE OTHER INGREDIENTS

1 tbsp groundnut oil
1 large cucumber
½ cup Thai basil leaves
8 rice papers

1 Put the block of tofu between layers of cotton kitchen towels and put it on a plate. Place a heavy plate or mortar pestle on top of it for 15–20 minutes so that all the moisture from the tofu is pressed out.

2 Mix all the ingredients for the marinade in a bowl.

3 Cut the tofu into 8 sticks and marinate it in the prepared mix for 15–20 minutes.

4 Put the peanut oil in a pan over moderate heat.

5 Shake off excess marinade from the tofu sticks and shallow-fry them on both sides, till golden and crisp. Remove and keep aside.

6 Peel the cucumber and cut it in half lengthwise. Remove and discard the seeds.

7 Cut the cucumber flesh into sticks.

8 Peel the carrot and cut it into sticks.

9 Lightly coat the cucumber and carrot sticks in the leftover marinade.

TO PREPARE THE ROLLS

1 Line a chopping board with a damp (but not soaking) kitchen towel.

2 Keep a deep dish filled with lukewarm water handy.

3 Dip each rice paper in the water for 10–15 seconds.

4 Place it on the towel-lined board and arrange 1 tofu stick, a few sticks of cucumber and carrot and a few basil leaves on the lower third of the circle.

5 Bring the two sides to the centre, fold the lower part upwards and then roll the entire rice paper roll upwards to close the roll from all sides.

6 Serve with a satay sauce for dipping.

Check p. 198 for a recipe that will make the perfect dipping sauce for these rolls.

Tofu contains phytoestrogen, a plant-based chemical that mimics the hormone oestrogen, due to which it is believed to prevent bone loss and ease other menopausal symptoms.

CALORIES (KCAL)	PROTEIN	FATS	CARBOHYDRATES	FIBRE
79.7	2.6	3.3	10.4	0.3

(per roll)

Soya Bengal Gram Kebabs

Tikkis or kebabs on a platter are a delight to serve. Make them small enough that they are barely one- or two-bite-sized pieces. Serve them with an assortment of chutneys and keep toothpicks handy for party starters that your guests will love. I make sure we have enough extras to roll up into rotis for breakfast.

MAKES
10–12 kebabs

THE DAL
½ cup chana dal, soaked overnight
½ tsp salt

THE SOYA NUGGETS
1 cup small soya nuggets
½ tsp salt

THE POTATO
1 small potato, boiled (approx. 60 g)
¾ tsp salt

THE OTHER INGREDIENTS
½ tsp green cardamom powder
½ tsp cinnamon powder
¼ tsp clove powder
¼ tsp freshly grated nutmeg
1 tsp freshly ground black pepper
½ tsp red chilli powder
10–12 cashew nut halves

THE DAL

1 Drain the dal and rinse well.

2 Put the dal into a pan with the salt and boil for 5–6 minutes, till just tender.

3 Drain thoroughly.

4 Transfer the dal into a mixer jar and pulse to get a coarse, dry puree. Remove into a bowl.

THE SOYA NUGGETS

1 Half fill a pan with water and bring to a boil with the salt over high heat.

2 Add the soya nuggets to the boiling water and allow to simmer for 2–3 minutes.

3 Drain the nuggets through a sieve, squeezing out every bit of moisture from them.

4 Pulse the nuggets in a mixer to a coarse consistency.

5 Add this to the crushed dal in the bowl. Mix to blend well.

THE POTATO

1 Peel the potato and mash it in another bowl with the salt.

2 Add it to the bowl containing the dal and soya nugget mix and blend it in.

TO FRY THE KEBABS

Ghee to shallow-fry

TO COMPLETE THE KEBABS

1 Add the spice powders to the bowl and knead to get a smooth dough.

2 Divide the dough into 10–12 portions and shape into patties, roughly 2" in diameter and ½" thick. Press a cashew nut half into the centre of each kebab.

3 Arrange on a dish.

4 Cover with cling film and refrigerate for a minimum of 30 minutes.

TO FRY THE KEBABS

1 Put 1–2 tbsp of ghee in a frying pan over low heat.

2 Shallow-fry the kebabs on each side for 6–7 minutes over low-to-moderate heat, till golden-brown and crisp.

TO SERVE

1 Drain the kebabs and arrange them on a serving platter.

2 Serve with any chutney of your choice or with tomato ketchup.

See photograph 35 of colour insert.

Take care not to overcook the dal, otherwise the kebab mix will be too soft and difficult to shape or fry.

If you don't have the spice powders mentioned in the recipe, lightly toast whole green cardamoms, cloves and cinnamon till aromatic. Once cooled, grind to a fine powder in a spice grinder and use this spice mix along with the other spices mentioned. For maximum flavour, though, nutmeg needs to be grated fresh.

You can add mashed sweet potato instead of potato but increase the spice powders by a pinch each to balance out the mild sweetness.

This same mixture can be used as a high-protein stuffing for parathas.

Ensure that the brand of soya nuggets you buy has a no-GMO label.

CALORIES (KCAL)	PROTEIN	FATS	CARBOHYDRATES	FIBRE
76.2	3.9	3.3	7.9	2.1

(per kebab)

Bengal Gram Hummus with Roasted Tomatoes

Hummus is one of the healthiest snacks out there. Classic hummus is made with cooked chickpeas and has the added goodness of tahini and extra-virgin olive oil. That, however, doesn't stop you from making hummus with any beans or lentils you can lay your hands on. I love roasting the profusion of seasonal cherry tomatoes from the garden till they are nearly charred and blending them with cooked beans to make a mouth-wateringly tart hummus.

MAKES

1½ cups (approx.)

THE DAL

¾ cup chana dal, soaked overnight or for a minimum of 6 hrs

A pinch of salt

THE TOMATOES

5 medium-sized tomatoes

4 cloves garlic, peeled

1 tbsp olive oil

A pinch of salt

THE OTHER INGREDIENTS

A pinch of salt

¼ tsp smoked paprika

TO SERVE

1 tbsp extra-virgin olive oil

THE DAL

1 Soak the dal overnight in plenty of water or for a minimum of 6 hours.

2 Drain the dal and rinse thoroughly.

3 Put the dal into a pressure cooker with 2 cups of water and a pinch of salt.

4 Close the pressure cooker with the lid and the pressure weight plugged in.

5 Keep the cooker over high heat till it reaches full pressure (first whistle).

6 Open the cooker after the pressure subsides.

7 Alternatively, boil the dal on the stovetop for 6–8 minutes, till just tender but not mushy.

8 Drain the cooked dal and keep aside. Reserve the cooking liquid for any other recipe (such as a rasam) if desired.

THE TOMATOES

1 Preheat the oven to 200°C.

2 Halve the tomatoes and arrange them on a small baking tray, along with the garlic cloves.

3 Rub 1 tbsp of olive oil over them and sprinkle a pinch of salt.

4 Put the tray in the centre of the oven and roast for 30–40 minutes at 200°C, till you see black blisters on the surface of the tomatoes.

5 Remove and allow to cool. Reserve any juices that are in the tray.

6 Peel the roasted tomatoes.

TO COMPLETE

1 Transfer the cooked dal to a mixer jar along with the tomatoes, garlic and the roasting juices. Season with a pinch of salt and the smoked paprika and blend to a smooth puree.

TO SERVE

1 Remove into a bowl and smoothen out the surface with the back of a spoon.

2 Drizzle the olive oil over the bowl of hummus and serve.

See photograph 3 of colour insert.

Roasting the tomatoes gives the hummus a unique flavour. Try roasting on the stovetop in a heavy-bottomed pan if you don't have access to an oven. The same can also be done in an air fryer by using a small tin that fits inside the air fryer basket.

Bengal gram or chana dal with a low glycaemic index – 20 grams protein per 100 grams of serving – is rich in insoluble fibre, which makes it one of the top foods for diabetics. It can be put to use in snacks, salads, dals, vegetable preparations and in pulaos.

CALORIES (KCAL)	PROTEIN	FATS	CARBOHYDRATES	FIBRE
627.6	21.6	31.2	68.4	21.6

(per 1½ cups)

Paneer and Bengal Gram Scramble (Bhurji)

This is the kind of recipe I resort to when I have a little bit of this and that languishing in the refrigerator and one final act of clean-up is much needed before ordering a fresh batch of produce. Spinach gives this dish a welcome burst of colour.

SERVES 4

THE TEMPERING

- 1 tbsp mustard oil
- ½ tsp cumin seeds (jeera)
- ¼ tsp mustard seeds
- A pinch of asafoetida powder (hing)
- 1 tsp finely diced fresh ginger
- 2–3 green chillies, finely chopped

THE OTHER INGREDIENTS

- 1 medium-sized onion, finely chopped
- ½ tsp turmeric powder
- 1 cup chopped spinach leaves
- 1 cup chana dal, cooked, but not mushy
- 1 cup crumbled paneer
- 2 tsp coriander powder
- ¾ tsp salt

THE TEMPERING

1 Heat the mustard oil in a frying pan over moderate heat until it begins smoking.

2 Stir in the cumin and mustard seeds along with the asafoetida powder.

3 When the seeds splutter, add the ginger and green chillies and fry for 1 minute over low heat.

TO COMPLETE

1 Add the onion and cook it over low-to-moderate heat for 5–6 minutes, till the onion is translucent. Mix in the turmeric powder and spinach leaves. Stir over high heat for 1 minute.

2 Reduce the heat and add the dal, paneer, coriander powder and salt. Toss gently without mashing up the dal and paneer too much.

TO SERVE

1 Finish with garam masala powder and coriander leaves, giving the dish a final stir to combine.

2 Serve hot with rotis.

TO SERVE

½ tsp garam masala powder

2–3 tbsp finely chopped fresh coriander leaves

Use any other greens instead of spinach. You can also use a larger quantity of coriander leaves and make them a part of the dish instead of just as a garnish.

Ensure that the dal is cooked but retains its shape and has a bite to it.

If you are not a fan of mustard oil, substitute it with any other oil of your choice.

CALORIES (KCAL)	PROTEIN	FATS	CARBOHYDRATES	FIBRE
190.5	8.9	11.8	12.4	3.2

(per serving)

Green Moong Crêpes with Caramelized Onions

The first time I heard of *pesarattu* was when I was in my early twenties. It was a recipe listed in the booklet that came along with a food processor. The idea of an almost instant batter that required no fermentation seemed genius for a newbie cook like me. Over the years I have tweaked this simple recipe in various ways, like this one. This particular recipe, for instance, is a flavour plus version of *pesarattu* with added fresh herbs such as mint and coriander. The addition of poha gives it a delightful texture.

Prepare a batch of sesame coconut podi (p. 184) to use as a topping on these crêpes.

MAKES
4 crêpes

THE CRÊPE BATTER
- 2 cups moong sprouts
- ½ cup fresh mint leaves
- ½ cup fresh coriander leaves
- 1 green chilli, roughly chopped
- 1 tsp fresh ginger, chopped
- ¼ cup red-rice poha (thin variety)
- ½ tsp salt

THE CARAMELIZED ONIONS
- 4 medium-sized onions
- 1 tbsp groundnut oil
- ½ tsp cumin seeds (jeera)

TO FRY THE CRÊPES
- 2 tbsp groundnut oil

THE CRÊPE BATTER

1 Wash the moong sprouts, drain and transfer to a blender jar.

2 Blend along with the herbs, green chilli, ginger, poha, salt and ¼ cup water, till you get a smooth batter.

3 Dilute with up to ¼ cup water to get a thick yet pouring consistency.

THE CARAMELIZED ONIONS

1 There is a generous stuffing of caramelized onions in each crêpe for which we need up to 1 medium-sized onion per crêpe.

2 Peel the onions, cut into half and slice fine.

3 Heat the oil in a frying pan.

4 Add the cumin seeds.

5 When they splutter, stir in the sliced onions.

6 Sauté the onions on low-to-moderate heat, till golden-brown. This process will easily take12–15 minutes for 4 onions.

7 Drain the remaining oil and keep aside.

TO SERVE

Sesame coconut spice mix or podi (p. 184) or any other spicy podi of choice

TO PREPARE THE CRÊPES

1 Place a tava over moderate heat and smear it with a few drops of oil, using kitchen paper.

2 When hot, spoon a ladle (approx. 1/3 cup) of batter on the tava and spread it out into a 5"–6" crêpe.

3 Cook over moderate heat to the desired crispness, using the remaining oil.

4 Flip over and cook the other side for 30 seconds or so.

5 Keep warm.

6 Repeat with the remaining batter.

TO SERVE

1 Spread the browned onions over one half of each crêpe.

2 Top with coconut sesame podi or any other spicy podi of your choice.

3 Fold over and serve hot.

For a shortcut, add finely chopped onions to the batter itself and then prepare the crêpes.

Instead of red rice poha you can also stir in ¼ cup red rice flour into the batter.

By all means, use the packed moong sprouts available in most supermarkets. Give them a good rinse before proceeding with the recipe.

Green moong beans have a powerful scavenging effect on free radicals, thereby exerting an anti-inflammatory effect.

CALORIES (KCAL)	PROTEIN	FATS	CARBOHYDRATES	FIBRE
155.0	3.1	10.0	14.5	2.4

(per crêpe)

Summer Yogurt Soup (Dahi ka Shorba)

When I was testing this recipe, I asked myself, 'So, how is this different from a *kadhi* or *moar kuzhambu*?'

When I tasted the shorba, though, I got my answer. This one is a very light soup, perfect to start summer lunches with. There are no tadka ingredients like curry leaves or chillies floating around, which makes it perfect for elegant shot glasses and a summer party!

SERVES 6

THE SHORBA
1 cup fresh yogurt
2 tsp rice flour
½ tsp salt
A small handful of fresh coriander leaves
A small handful of dill leaves (sua bhaji)

THE SPICE PASTE
½ tsp mustard seeds
½ tsp cumin seeds
2 tbsp grated fresh coconut
1 small green chilli, roughly chopped
1 sprig fresh, tender curry leaves

THE SHORBA

1 Whisk the yogurt, rice flour and salt in a bowl with 1 cup of water to get a smooth lump-free mixture.

2 Transfer this into a small pan and place over low heat.

3 Let it come to a simmer, stirring all the while to prevent the yogurt from splitting.

THE SPICE PASTE

1 Combine all the ingredients for the spice paste in a small mixer jar. Add 2–3 tbsp of the yogurt mix from the pan and grind to make a fine paste.

2 Scrape out the paste from the jar and whisk it into the shorba.

3 Bring it to a simmer again and continue to simmer for about 2 minutes, stirring all the while.

TO COMPLETE

1 Remove from heat and let it cool.

2 Transfer to a bowl and refrigerate for 2–3 hours.

3 Spoon into small cups or shot glasses and serve chilled.

See photograph 24 of colour insert.

In case the shorba separates, give it a quick whisk before serving it.

If you don't mind the traditional tadka, then by all means combine the fresh coconut into the shorba and temper the remaining ingredients for the paste in hot oil. Pour this over the shorba just before serving.

The same dish can be made into a thicker kadhi by whisking in 2 tbsp of gram flour (besan) instead of rice flour and proceeding with the recipe as is. Serve hot instead of chilled though.

Setting yogurt in small cup-sized storage containers makes it a go-to snack.

As per a study, consumption of whole-fat yogurt brings about a reduction in waist circumference and abdominal fat.

CALORIES (KCAL)	PROTEIN	FATS	CARBOHYDRATES	FIBRE
49.3	1.7	3.2	3.4	0.7

(per serving)

Paneer in Banana Leaf Parcels (Paneer Paturi)

The technique for this recipe is inspired from Bengali cuisine where chenna or veggies, topped with mustard sauce and wrapped in banana leaf parcels are pan-cooked to deliciousness. The green 'chutney' used in this recipe is inspired from a Yemeni hot sauce called *skhug*, which is prepared in both red and green versions. The original green *skhug* is made with coriander leaves, parsley, cumin, cardamom, chillies and garlic, with a douse of extra-virgin olive oil. My version gets its lush herbaceous flavour from dill and coriander leaves, with coconut and rice flour being the Bengali additions. The *skhug*-smothered paneer in banana leaf parcels makes it a unique dish and a super quick one too.

SERVES 4

THE PANEER

- 200 g paneer
- 1 tsp fresh ginger, grated
- 2 tsp coriander powder
- ¼ tsp salt

THE GREEN CHUTNEY

- ½ cup dill leaves (sua bhaji)
- ½ cup fresh coriander leaves
- 4 cloves garlic
- 2–3 green chillies, to taste
- 1 tsp cumin seeds (jeera)
- 2 tbsp fresh coconut, grated
- 1½ tsp rice flour
- ½ tsp salt
- 2 tsp mustard oil

THE PANEER

1 Grate or crumble the paneer into a large bowl.

2 Add the ginger, coriander powder and salt and combine together with some heavy-duty kneading, till you get a very smooth mixture.

3 Divide into 8 portions and keep aside.

THE GREEN CHUTNEY

1 Combine all the ingredients for the chutney in a small mixer jar and blend to get a smooth paste.

THE PARCELS

1 Put a tava over moderate heat.

2 Heat the banana leaf squares over the hot tava on both sides so that they are lightly scorched and pliable. This is to prevent them from tearing when folding the parcels.

3 Place a portion of the paneer mixture over a square of banana leaf and flatten lightly.

4 Top with 1 tsp of green chutney.

THE PARCELS

8 x 6" squares of banana leaves or foil

2 tsp mustard oil

5 Fold the banana leaf over the paneer to make a sealed parcel and secure with toothpicks or twine. Prepare the remaining parcels in the same way.

6 Coat the same tava with a thin film of oil. Place the parcels on the hot tava, turning them over after 3–4 minutes.

7 Remove from heat.

TO SERVE

1 Open the parcels just before serving with steamed rice or rotis.

See photograph 37 of colour insert.

If you are not a fan of mustard oil, use any other cold-pressed oil.

Use foil or heavy-duty parchment paper to make the parcels if you can't find banana leaves.

Use a mix of parboiled or blanched veggies instead of paneer to make it a vegan dish.

Homemade soft set/crumbled paneer can be used for this recipe instead of the store-bought blocks.

Dill is known for its hypoglycaemic effects and it has been reported to reduce the incidence of diabetic complications.

CALORIES (KCAL)	PROTEIN	FATS	CARBOHYDRATES	FIBRE
205.5	9.9	16.0	5.6	1.5

(per serving)

Almost Salad: Fresh Green Bengal Gram

Stocking up on cooked green chickpeas (chana) in the refrigerator means you have one healthy ingredient to add to salads and curries or to serve as a teatime snack like this one. This recipe has the taste spectrum of a chaat with the health benefits of a salad.

SERVES 3–4

THE SALAD

- 1½ cups cooked green chickpeas (approx. ½ cup uncooked)
- 1 large potato, boiled, peeled and cubed
- ¼ tsp black salt
- 2 tbsp any green chutney of choice
- ¼ cup finely chopped onion
- ¼ cup fresh pomegranate arils
- ½ cup seedless green grapes
- ½ a lemon, juiced
- ¼ cup finely chopped fresh coriander leaves
- ½ tsp chaat masala
- 1 tbsp tamarind chutney, homemade or store-bought

TO SERVE

- 1 lemon, cut into wedges
- ½ tsp chaat masala

THE SALAD

1 Toss the green chana, potato, black salt and green chutney in bowl, till the gram and potatoes are well coated.

2 Add the onion and pomegranate arils and mix well.

3 Halve the green grapes and mix them in.

4 Squeeze the lemon juice over the chaat.

5 Top with coriander leaves, chaat masala powder and tamarind chutney and toss well to combine.

TO SERVE

1 Divide the chaat between 3–4 plates.

2 Sprinkle chaat masala powder on top and serve with a wedge of lemon.

Cooked chickpeas (kabuli chana) as well as brown chickpeas (kala chana) make good substitutes for green chana. Boiled sweet potato can be used instead of potato.

Keep a bottle of green chutney (see p. 43) in the refrigerator to prepare such dishes at a moment's notice. Store-bought tamarind chutney adds the essential sweet-sour flavour to chaats. Buy a bottle and it stays in the refrigerator for months.

Sprinkle crushed roasted peanuts over the chaat to provide crunch minus any deep-fried additions that also adds a dose of healthy fats.

 *Chickpeas are rich in vitamin B6, manganese and magnesium that help reduce PMS (premenstrual syndrome) symptoms.*

CALORIES (KCAL)	PROTEIN	FATS	CARBOHYDRATES	FIBRE
100.6	3.2	0.9	20.9	3.4

(per serving)

Green Apple Rasam

My uncle, Raju Chitapa, is known for his kitchen experiments. He once made rasam with apples because there were no tomatoes at home. I'm sure he was promptly chided by my aunt for wasting expensive apples in a rasam, but I loved his idea because the green apple adds a gentle sweetness and tartness to the rasam, making it perfect to sip before your meal. This is more of an appetizer rasam than a main course rasam that is eaten with rice.

SERVES 4–6

¼ cup arhar or tur dal, soaked for 30 minutes
¼ tsp turmeric powder
1 green apple
¾ tsp salt
1 tsp rasam powder (see cooking notes)
1 tbsp lemon juice

THE GARNISH
1 tbsp finely chopped fresh coriander leaves

THE TEMPERING
1 tbsp ghee
½ tsp cumin seeds (jeera)
1 sprig fresh curry leaves

1 Drain the soaked dal and rinse well.

2 Put it in a pressure cooker with 2 cups of water and the turmeric powder.

3 Core the apple and cut it into chunks with the peel.

4 Add it to the cooker.

5 Close the pressure cooker with the lid and the pressure weight plugged in.

6 Cook on high for 2 whistles. Lower the heat and cook for 12 more minutes, so that the dal is cooked to a smooth paste.

7 Open the cooker after the pressure subsides.

8 Transfer the contents of the cooker into a blender.

9 Once cool enough, blend to a smooth puree with an extra ½ cup of water.

10 Pass the puree through a fine-meshed sieve, pressing out all the juices with the back of a ladle. Return the rasam to the pressure cooker.

11 Season with salt and rasam powder.

12 Simmer this over low heat without the lid.

13 Remove into a serving bowl.

14 Stir in the lemon juice and garnish with coriander leaves.

THE TEMPERING

1 Heat the ghee in a small pan or tempering ladle.

2 Add the cumin seeds and curry leaves.

3 As soon as the seeds, splutter pour the contents of the pan over the rasam.

4 Stir well and serve in small glasses.

See photograph 23 of colour insert.

Use ready-made rasam powder of known South Indian brands or prepare your own by lightly roasting 1 tsp arhar or tur dal, 2 dried red chillies, 1 tsp cumin seeds and 8 black peppercorns and grinding to a fine powder.

Try this recipe using pineapple instead of apple for another appetising fruity rasam.

A study found that having a low-calorie soup before a main meal can cut down on the quantity and calories consumed in the meal, thereby aiding weight loss.

CALORIES (KCAL)	PROTEIN	FATS	CARBOHYDRATES	FIBRE
88.6	3.0	2.6	13.4	2.6

(per serving)

Paneer with Spinach and Fenugreek Greens (Palak Methi Paneer)

Prepare this dish in the winter when the paneer is creamy and the fenugreek greens are at their freshest. The nut paste gives the dish a creaminess that offsets the bitter tinge from the greens quite nicely.

SERVES 4

THE CASHEW PASTE

- 2 tbsp cashew pieces, halved
- 1 tbsp melon seeds
- 1 tbsp poppy seeds (khus-khus)

THE PANEER AND GREENS

- 200 g paneer
- A pinch of salt
- 1 medium-sized bunch of spinach (approx. 200 g)
- 2 cups fenugreek leaves (methi)

THE TEMPERING

- 2 tbsp groundnut oil
- ¼ tsp fenugreek seeds
- ½ tsp mustard seeds
- ½ tsp cumin seeds (jeera)
- 1 tsp grated fresh ginger
- 6–8 cloves garlic, finely chopped
- 3 green chillies, slit lengthwise

THE CASHEW PASTE

1 Soak the cashews, melon seeds and poppy seeds in a cup of hot water for 30 minutes.

2 Drain and grind to a smooth paste.

THE PANEER AND GREENS

1 Cut the paneer into ¾" cubes and immerse them in a bowl of hot water with a pinch of salt for 5–10 minutes.

2 Remove and squeeze out the excess water gently. Keep aside.

3 Pluck out the leaves and tender stems from the spinach. Wash, clean, chop fine and keep aside. Reserve the fenugreek leaves in a bowl of cold water.

THE TEMPERING

1 Heat the oil in a frying pan.

2 Add the fenugreek seeds, mustard seeds and cumin seeds.

3 When they start to splutter, stir in the ginger, garlic and green chillies.

4 Sauté for 30 seconds, till aromatic.

TO COMPLETE

1 Reduce the heat and add the onions.

2 Sauté with a pinch of salt for 4–5 minutes, till translucent.

3 Remove the fenugreek leaves from the bowl of water, gently squeeze out excess water and chop finely.

THE OTHER INGREDIENTS

1 large onion, finely sliced

¾ tsp salt

½ tsp garam masala powder

4 Add the fenugreek leaves and the spinach to the pan.

5 Stir over high heat for a minute or so, till the greens have wilted.

6 Mix in the cashew nut paste.

7 Dilute with ¼ cup water or more and simmer over moderate heat for 5–6 minutes.

8 Add the paneer cubes and toss, till well coated.

9 Sprinkle ½ tsp salt and the garam masala powder and stir to combine.

10 Bring to a simmer and cook for 2–3 minutes.

TO SERVE

1 Remove from heat and spoon into a serving bowl.

2 Serve hot with rotis.

Green leafy vegetables can be prepped over weekends and frozen in 1 cup portions in re-sealable bags for quick use on busy days.

Paneer is a good source of protein for lactovegetarians (18 grams per 100 grams of serving). Additionally, it is a calcium-rich food (200 grams per 100 grams of serving), which is half the daily requirement for adults and children 9 years and older.

GARDENING TIP:

Methi is one of the easiest greens to grow in pots. Soak methi seeds in water for 12 hours. Drain and allow to sprout for a day or two. Sow the methi sprouts in compost rich soil in pots in a single layer. In around two weeks you can snip the leaves for use. The stems will sprout more leaves in a few days.

CALORIES (KCAL)	PROTEIN	FATS	CARBOHYDRATES	FIBRE
252.9	13.5	18.5	8.0	3.3

(per serving)

Indian Gooseberry, Carrot and Pomegranate in Yogurt (Amla, Gajar and Anar Raita)

Raita, a yogurt-based salad, is a very common accompaniment to an Indian meal – cucumber, boondi and onion raita being the usual suspects. Amla or Indian gooseberry raita is common in traditional Tamil cuisine where gooseberries preserved in brine are crushed and added to yogurt, topped with a tempering of chillies, urad dal and curry leaves. This recipe has a few more additions that make it an appealing accompaniment to any meal.

SERVES 4

- 2 cups fresh yogurt
- 2 tsp urad dal flour
- 4 Indian gooseberries (amla)
- ½ tsp salt
- ¼ tsp turmeric powder
- 1 medium-sized carrot
- ¼ cup fresh pomegranate arils

THE TEMPERING

- 2 tsp groundnut oil
- ½ tsp mustard seeds
- 2 tsp urad dal
- 1 sprig fresh curry leaves
- 1–2 dried red chillies or fresh green chillies

1 In a bowl, whisk the yogurt with the flour till well combined.

2 In a small pressure cooker, combine the amla with salt, turmeric powder and ½ a cup of water.

3 Close the pressure cooker with the lid and the pressure weight plugged in.

4 Cook the amla for 5–6 minutes over low heat after the cooker reaches full pressure (first whistle).

5 Open the cooker after the pressure subsides.

6 Remove the amla from the cooker and separate into quarters, discarding the stone.

7 Peel the carrot and chop it into small chunks.

8 Blend the cooked amla and carrot in a mixer jar to get a coarse paste.

9 Stir it into the yogurt.

10 Mix in the pomegranate.

11 Transfer to a serving bowl.

THE GARNISH

1–2 tsp finely chopped fresh coriander leaves (optional)

THE TEMPERING

1 Heat the oil in a small pan or a tempering ladle.

2 Add all the ingredients for the tempering in the order given.

3 Once the mustard seeds splutter and the dal turns golden-brown, pour the contents of the pan over the raita.

TO SERVE

1 Garnish with fresh coriander leaves if desired and serve.

See photograph 34 of colour insert.

Urad dal flour gives a thickness to homemade yogurt while also lending a nutty flavour. This flour is available in many supermarkets. You can also prepare it at home by lightly toasting ¼ cup of urad dal for 5–6 minutes and, once cool, grinding it to a fine powder.

When amla is not in season, use 2 tsp of amla murabba (a preserve). Choose a brand that uses jaggery instead of sugar.

The antioxidant content of a food is measured in Oxygen Radical Absorbance Capacity (ORAC) units. Amla or the Indian gooseberry has an impressive ORAC score of 2,61,500 – especially when compared to blueberries that have an ORAC score of 4,669.

CALORIES (KCAL)	PROTEIN	FATS	CARBOHYDRATES	FIBRE
120.2	5.0	6.4	11.2	2.3

(per serving)

Eggs and Veggies

Give me eggs for any meal of the day and I'm a happy camper. In this recipe I've used vegetables that you'll almost always find in your kitchen – potatoes and onions from the pantry, green peas from the freezer and instead of green bell pepper, use any bits or bobs of veggies you find in the crisper of your refrigerator. Make a large pan full of these eggs and veggies by increasing the quantities of ingredients and you have one dish taken care of for a Sunday brunch.

SERVES 2

- 4 eggs
- 1 tbsp ghee or oil
- ¼ tsp turmeric powder
- ½ tsp cumin seeds (jeera)
- 1 medium-sized onion, halved and sliced
- ½ cup green peas
- 1 medium-sized potato, peeled and finely diced
- 1 medium-sized green bell pepper, finely diced
- ¾ tsp salt
- ¼ tsp freshly ground black pepper

THE GARNISH

- Salt and freshly ground black pepper
- 1 tsp of sesame coconut podi or any fresh herbs of choice (optional)

1 Place the eggs in a medium-sized pan. Cover with water and place over high heat. Bring to a boil. Once the water is on a rolling boil, turn off the heat.

2 Cover with a well-fitting lid and keep aside for 10 minutes.

3 Remove the eggs with a slotted spoon and plunge them into a bowl of cold water. Peel and cut the eggs into quarters and keep aside.

4 Heat the ghee in a large frying pan over moderate heat.

5 Stir in the turmeric powder and cumin seeds.

6 When the cumin seeds splutter, add all the chopped vegetables and the peas.Toss over high heat for 1–2 minutes. Cover and cook for 6–8 minutes, till the potatoes and peas are tender.

7 Season with salt and pepper and stir to combine.

8 Divide between two bowls and top with quartered eggs.

9 Sprinkle salt and pepper over the eggs if required.

10 Garnish with the sesame coconut podi (p. 184) or fresh herbs.

See photograph 32 of colour insert.

This is my favourite method to get perfect hard-boiled eggs with bright yellow yolks and no grey sulphur ring. I learnt this trick from Mark Bittman's cookbooks.

If you like, you can even scramble the eggs along with the vegetables, but scrambled eggs need to be consumed right away or they are not very palatable.

Eggs make a complete protein. Protein, fibre, vitamin and minerals from this single dish keeps you full for 4–5 hours. Try and source organic eggs.

CALORIES (KCAL)	PROTEIN	FATS	CARBOHYDRATES	FIBRE
316.0	16.6	17.8	22.1	4.9

(per serving)

Green Eggs with Jalapeños and Olives

Green eggs inspired by Dr Seuss, minus the ham! The inspiration for this dish comes from one of my favourite eating spots in Bengaluru – Red Fork. A generous portion of green scrambled eggs piled up high on a hunk of a sourdough toast, topped with fresh salad greens and a drizzle of basil oil is my favourite dish from their blackboard menu and I love recreating it in my kitchen for leisurely weekend breakfasts.

SERVES 2–3

- 6 eggs
- ¼ cup milk
- ½ tsp salt
- ½ tsp freshly ground black pepper
- 1 tbsp olive oil
- 1 cup spinach, finely chopped
- ¼ cup fresh basil leaves, chopped
- 2–3 jalapeños, fresh or in brine, sliced
- 2 tbsp sliced pitted green olives

THE GARNISH

- ¼ cup grated Parmesan cheese

TO SERVE

- Whole-grain toasts

1 Crack the eggs into a large bowl and whisk well along with the milk, salt and black pepper.

2 Heat the oil in a frying pan. Sauté the spinach and basil leaves over high heat for 20–30 seconds, till wilted.

3 Lower the heat and add the eggs.

4 Swirl around with a spatula, scraping the base of the pan and making figure of 8 motions for 5–6 minutes, till the eggs are scrambled but still moist.

5 Stir in the jalapeños and green olives.

TO SERVE

1 Spoon scrambled eggs on to a platter.

2 Sprinkle grated Parmesan cheese on top.

3 Serve with wholegrain toasts as a part of brunch.

In the absence of jalapeños, use finely sliced green chillies.

Cooking eggs over low heat ensures that you get soft scrambled eggs that are not rubbery in texture. Some chefs even advocate scrambling them over indirect heat in a double boiler.

The spicy nature of jalapeños or any other variety of chillies comes from the chemical capsaicin, which is said to have pain-relieving properties.

GARDENING TIP:

Basil can be easily grown in pots in a sunny windowsill. Start by using seeds or saplings. They grow best in warm weather when there's plenty of sunlight. Keep pruning the top 2-3 leaves regularly for a bushy plant. Once the plant begins flowering, it will stop producing leaves.

CALORIES (KCAL)	PROTEIN	FATS	CARBOHYDRATES	FIBRE
267.6	16.8	21.1	4.8	1.0

(per serving)

Baked Egg Cups

Kids love this egg breakfast dish served in individual cup-sized portions. Topped with colourful vegetables, time-saving and pretty on the dining table – this breakfast ticks all the boxes.

MAKES
6 eggs cups

THE EGGS
4 eggs
¼ cup milk
½ tsp salt
½ tsp freshly ground black pepper

THE VEGETABLES
1 tbsp olive oil
½ cup diced red bell pepper
½ cup diced green bell pepper
1 medium-sized onion, finely chopped
¼ cup green peas
1 tsp mixed dried herbs
A pinch of salt

THE TOPPING
4–5 tbsp grated Cheddar cheese
½ tsp paprika powder or smoked paprika

1 Line a 6-cup large-sized muffin tin with silicon moulds or thick paper casings. Brush the moulds with a few drops of oil.

2 Preheat the oven to 190°C.

THE EGGS

1 Whisk the eggs, milk, salt and pepper in a bowl.

2 Divide this mixture between the 6 muffin moulds.

THE VEGETABLES

1 Heat the olive oil in a frying pan.

2 Sauté the bell peppers, onion and green peas with the salt for 3–4 minutes over moderate heat, till half-cooked.

3 Sprinkle the herbs over the vegetables and give them a final toss.

4 Divide into 6 portions and top over the egg mixture.

TO COMPLETE

1 Sprinkle with the cheese and paprika powder.

2 Bake in the centre of the preheated oven for 15 minutes at 180°C for fully set eggs.

3 Serve hot as a part of a brunch or pack in a paper bag for a portable breakfast.

For a slightly more elaborate version, cut out 3"-diameter circles from tortillas. Moisten them slightly and line each muffin tin with these tortillas. Brush lightly with oil and proceed with the same recipe, filling these tortilla cups with the egg mixture. Leftover parathas can also be used for this purpose.

Green bell peppers, while rich in vitamin C, are a good source of the antioxidant zeaxanthin which prevents oxidative damage to the retina. Bell peppers are also a very good source of thiamine (vitamin B1), one serving providing over half the daily requirement. Thiamine, along with the other B vitamins, is necessary to convert carbohydrates into glucose, apart from its role in fat and protein metabolism.

CALORIES (KCAL)	PROTEIN	FATS	CARBOHYDRATES	FIBRE
117.5	6.5	8.2	5.5	1.5

(per egg cup)

Curried Moth Bean Sprouts (Matki)

Matki or moth beans are a very underrated ingredient. They sprout beautifully in 24–48 hours, cook quickly and, for their tiny size, pack quite a bit of flavour, which for some is an acquired taste. Maharashtrians put them to good use in *usal*. This is my go-to recipe for matki sprouts which goes really well with dosas. For another delicious way to use this curry, see the cooking notes on the next page. Please note that this recipe involves sprouting the moth beans for 2 days.

SERVES 4

THE SPROUTS

1/3 cup moth beans (matki)
¼ tsp turmeric powder
A pinch of asafoetida powder (hing)
½ tsp salt

THE SPICE PASTE

1 tbsp coriander seeds
1 tsp cumin seeds
2 dried red chillies
2 tbsp fresh coconut scrapings
1 large tomato, roughly chopped
2 cloves garlic, roughly chopped
½" piece fresh ginger, sliced

THE TEMPERING

2 tsp groundnut oil
¼ tsp mustard seeds
1 sprig fresh curry leaves

THE SPROUTS

1 Soak the moth beans overnight or for 6–8 hours in plenty of water.

2 Drain and place in a glass jar or container, leaving the lid slightly open.

3 After 24 hours wash the sprouts, drain and keep for sprouting again in the same jar.

4 This process will give you roughly 1½ cups of delicate ½-inch long sprouts.

5 Bring 1 cup of water to a boil in a medium-sized pan.

6 Add the turmeric powder, asafoetida powder and ½ tsp salt to the water.

7 Add the sprouted moth beans and cook uncovered for 10 minutes over moderate heat, till the sprouts are cooked but retain their shape.

THE SPICE PASTE

1 Toast the coriander seeds, cumin seeds and red chillies in a small pan for 4–5 minutes over low heat.

2 Remove and allow to cool.

3 Grind the toasted ingredients with the remaining ingredients to make a fine paste.

THE OTHER INGREDIENTS

1 medium-sized onion, thinly sliced
¼ tsp salt
½ tsp garam masala powder

THE TEMPERING

1 Heat the oil in a frying pan.

2 Add the mustard seeds and curry leaves.

TO COMPLETE

1 When the seeds splutter, add the onions with a pinch of salt. Sauté for 6–8 minutes till they become translucent.

2 Add the ground spice paste and fry over moderate heat for around 8 minutes, till most of the liquid has evaporated.

3 Add the cooked sprouts along with the cooking liquid (if any).

4 Dilute with around ¼ cup water if required and simmer for 2 minutes.

TO SERVE

1 Finish with a sprinkle of garam masala powder.

2 Stir through and remove into a serving bowl.

3 Serve with hot dosas or rotis.

See photograph 36 of colour insert.

I love to make an Indian-style sprouts bowl with a serving of this curry, a ladle of cooked grains such as millet, rice or quinoa, and a dollop of yogurt. Top with finely chopped fresh coriander leaves and a spoonful of Maharashtrian garlic chutney.

Anti-nutrients such as tannins present in dried beans are eliminated by soaking and sprouting them. Make sure you use clean, filtered water for sprouting. Store-bought sprouts are best used in cooked dishes and not in salads.

CALORIES (KCAL)	PROTEIN	FATS	CARBOHYDRATES	FIBRE
78.4	1.9	4.7	7.6	2.5

(per serving)

Superfruit Salad with Black-Eyed Peas

Black-eyed peas, cowpeas or lobia are known for their role in hearty dishes like curries, stews and pots of chilli. They are definitely not known to make glamorous appearances. By pairing black-eyed peas with a medley of brightly coloured seasonal fruits, this salad defies stereotypes. Cape gooseberries come with their own papery cape which is why I have cheekily labelled it a 'superfruit'. They are available during a short window in April so make sure you get them and try this salad.

SERVES 2

THE SALAD

1 cup cooked black-eyed peas (lobia)
2 handfuls of seedless green grapes
8–10 cape gooseberries (rasbhari)
1 red apple

THE DRESSING

1 lemon, zested and juiced
2 tbsp extra-virgin olive oil
¼ tsp salt
¼ tsp freshly ground black pepper
2 tsp honey

THE GARNISH

2 tbsp coarsely chopped walnuts
A few sprigs of fresh dill leaves (sua bhaji)
50 g feta or blue cheese, crumbled

THE SALAD

1. Put the cooked black-eyed peas in a large salad bowl.
2. Halve the green grapes and cape gooseberries and add them to the bowl.
3. Scrub and wash the apple well. Keeping the peel intact adds to the colour and fibre quotient of the salad but, if you wish to, you can remove the peel and then dice into ½" cubes.
4. Toss along with the other ingredients in the bowl.

THE DRESSING

1. Combine all the dressing ingredients in a small bowl.
2. Whisk vigorously until thick and creamy.
3. Pour the dressing over the salad in the bowl.
4. Toss till the salad is well-coated with the dressing.

TO SERVE

1. Lightly toast the walnut pieces in a small pan over low heat for 3–4 minutes and allow to cool.
2. Top the salad with sprigs of dill, crumbled feta or blue cheese and toasted walnut pieces.

See photograph 38 of colour insert.

If you have some cape gooseberries left over, do try the Not Your Usual Kachumber recipe on p. 30.

If you can't find cape gooseberries, use a mix of black and seedless green grapes.

Black-eyed peas are a good source of iron for vegetarians. Half a cup (cooked) provides 25 per cent of the daily iron requirement for women and almost a third for men.

GARDENING TIP:

You can grow dill in pots with a depth of more than 12 inches. They need to be kept in full sun and watered lightly. Pinch off the growing tips regularly, just like basil, to get a bushier plant. Flowers and seeds shorten the growing life of dill.

CALORIES (KCAL)	PROTEIN	FATS	CARBOHYDRATES	FIBRE
371.2	12.7	18.1	42.0	4.7

(per serving)

Mixed Lentils with Malabar Spinach

Basella alba and *Basella rubra* are the two varieties of Malabar spinach, the *rubra* being the one with reddish-purple stalks. The taste and texture of these leaves is quite different from spinach. This easy-growing vine with fleshy, mucilaginous leaves makes a graceful addition to a window sill or kitchen garden. I don't recommend Malabar spinach for salads or smoothies but they do well in curries and dals.

SERVES 4

THE DALS

1 cup mixed dals (arhar or tur, chana, masoor, moong dal)
½ tsp turmeric powder

THE TEMPERING

1 tbsp ghee or oil
A pinch of asafoetida powder (hing)
1 tsp cumin seeds (jeera)

THE OTHER INGREDIENTS

1 tbsp ginger-garlic paste, freshly made
3–4 green chillies, slit
1 medium-sized onion, sliced
1 tsp salt
2 cups chopped Malabar spinach leaves
3 medium-sized tomatoes, pureed
2 tsp coriander powder

THE DALS

1 Wash the dals and soak them in water for 30 minutes.

2 Drain and place in a pressure cooker with a 4 litre or higher capacity along with 2½ cups of water and the turmeric powder.

3 Close the pressure cooker with the lid and the pressure weight plugged in.

4 Cook over high heat for 3 whistles. Lower the heat and cook for 10 minutes longer on sim.

5 Open the cooker after the pressure subsides.

THE TEMPERING

1 Meanwhile, heat the ghee or oil in a frying pan.

2 Stir in the asafoetida powder and cumin seeds.

THE CURRY

1 When the seeds splutter, add the ginger-garlic paste and green chillies. Fry for a few seconds.

2 Add the onions with a pinch of salt and fry over moderate heat for 6–8 minutes, till translucent.

3 Stir in the Malabar spinach and sauté over high heat for 3–4 minutes, till it has completely wilted.

½ tsp red chilli powder
1 tsp garam masala powder

THE GARNISH
2 tbsp chopped fresh coriander leaves

4 Add the tomatoes and bring to a simmer along with the spice powders and remaining salt.

5 Mix in the cooked dals and simmer for 2 minutes.

TO SERVE

1 Garnish with coriander leaves and serve with steamed rice, millets or rotis.

Malabar spinach is called mayalu *in Marathi,* poi shak *in Bengali and* basale soppu *in Kannada. It is also used in South East Asian cuisines.*

Use tamarind pulp or kokum instead of tomato puree as a souring agent for the dal.

The dish can also be prepared with a mix of split green moong, split black gram (urad) and kidney beans (rajmah) for a heartier dish. Do note that pressure cooking times will increase accordingly.

Malabar spinach fares well in the protein department (2.8 grams per 100 grams of serving). It is an excellent source of calcium and iron, three times the calcium and ten times the iron in spinach! Chewing on the mucilaginous leaves is said to provide relief to mouth ulcers.

GARDENING TIP:
Get a cutting of Malabar spinach vine or you can even use one of the stems from the store bought spinach. Keep in a glass of water for a week or so until it gives out tiny shoots. Plant in compost-rich soil. This quick growing vine will start sprouting a regular supply of leaves in 2–3 weeks.

CALORIES (KCAL)	PROTEIN	FATS	CARBOHYDRATES	FIBRE
194.5	10.8	3.6	29.7	6.5

(per serving)

healthy fats

Fat is a calorie-dense macronutrient that adds flavour to food and keeps you full after a meal. Fats are essential for the absorption of fat soluble vitamins, that is, vitamins A, E, D and K. In fact, Omega-3 fatty acids not only prevent heart disease, but also play a role in blood clotting and building cell membranes in the brain.

There are certain categories of fat that you must know about:

- **Unsaturated fats:** These fats are liquid at room temperature. Also called healthy fats or good fats, their consumption improves the cholesterol profile and reduces inflammation. Unsaturated fats in vegetarian diets can be gained from olive oil, groundnut oil, avocados, olives, almonds, peanuts, pistachios, flaxseed, soybean, leafy vegetables, chia seeds, etc. These should be the bulk of your fat consumption.
- **Saturated fats:** Mainly obtained from animal produce (including dairy), saturated fats are also found in some plant-based foods such as coconut, coconut oil and palm oil. The verdict on the consumption of saturated fats is still controversial. While studies have proven that eating more polyunsaturated fats in place of saturated fats can lower the risk of heart disease, there is no direct evidence connecting consumption of saturated fats like coconut oil or full fat yogurt to any negative heath repercussions. Hence, it's best to enjoy these in moderation.
- **Trans fats:** These are man-made fats obtained by processing vegetable oils into semi-solid fats by hydrogenation. Stick margarine, vanaspati, shortening used in mass-produced baked goods are some examples of trans fats. Repeated reheating of cooking oils, as is common in commercial deep-frying, turns them into trans fats. They are notorious for raising bad cholesterol (LDL) and lowering good cholesterol (HDL) and are linked to heart disease and inflammatory diseases. Avoid this category of fats completely.

There are conflicting opinions on the right percentage of fat in a diet. Generally, for men, a minimum of 15 per cent to a maximum of 30–35 per cent of the total calories in a day should be from fat. The recommendation for women in the reproductive age group is 20 per cent.

Different oils have different fatty acid compositions. It is, therefore, good to use a mix of oils in day-to-day cooking to get a variety of nutrients. Using groundnut oil, mustard oil, sesame (gingelly) oil, coconut oil and ghee in a variety of Indian dishes for daily cooking, butter and olive oil in Western cooking and extra-virgin olive oil for salads is a good mix to rely on.

All recipes in this book use cold-pressed oils (groundnut, mustard, coconut) which have better nutritional values and antioxidant levels, and more flavour. Try not to heat these oils to a very high temperature while cooking to prevent any degradation. Salads are also wonderful carriers of healthy fats, be it by way of nuts, seeds, leafy greens or the dressing. Seeds such as sesame, flax, niger can be prepared into *podis* (spice mixes) that can be had with rice or served with breakfast dishes. In addition to this section, check out the recipes for salad dressing in the 'Eat the Rainbow' section to include more healthy fats in your diet.

My Special Sesame-Coconut Spice Mix (Podi)

Molaga podi or gun powder is the standard accompaniment with idlis and dosas in Tamil homes. This crunchy, spicy *podi* with the addition of roasted sesame seeds and coconut is adapted from my maternal grandmother's recipe.

MAKES

1½ cups of *podi*

THE *PODI*

- ½ cup urad dal
- ¼ cup chana dal
- ¼ cup black sesame seeds
- ¼ cup white sesame seeds
- ¾ cup desiccated coconut
- ¼ cup raw peanuts
- 2 tsp coconut oil
- 10 dried red chillies (bedgi chillies)
- 1½–2 tsp salt

TO ROAST THE INGREDIENTS

1 Place a heavy-bottomed frying pan over moderate heat and dry-roast the ingredients in batches.

2 Start with the urad dal and the chana dal, stirring continuously till they turn deeply aromatic and golden-brown but definitely not to the point where they start smelling burnt. This should take 7–8 minutes. Transfer to a dish and allow to cool.

3 Now roast the black and white sesame seeds. As soon as the seeds hit the hot pan they will start popping. Keep stirring so that the seeds don't burn until the popping frequency reduces. You will also get an oily, toasty aroma. Transfer this to the same plate as the dals and allow to cool.

4 Toast the desiccated coconut in the same pan over low-to-moderate heat for 5–6 minutes, stirring all the while, till you get a rich aroma and the coconut turns dark golden-brown. Remove into a bowl to cool.

5 Next, roast the peanuts for 6–8 minutes over moderate heat, till they change colour. (To save some time, you can also do this step in the microwave while roasting the other ingredients. Spread the peanuts in a glass dish and microwave on high for 4–5 minutes.)

6 Add the coconut oil to the pan and throw in the red chillies. It will be good to turn on the exhaust fan in your kitchen at this point, as roasting chillies may irritate the eyes and throat. Fry the chillies

31. Chickpea Za'atar Croquettes

33: Tulsi *Thogayal* with Green Rice-Flour Dumplings

34: Indian Gooseberry, Carrot and Pomegranate in Yogurt (Amla, Gajar and Anar Raita)

35: Soya Bengal Gram Kebabs

36: Curried Moth Bean Sprouts (Matki)

37: Paneer in Banana Leaf Parcels (Paneer *Paturi*)

38: Superfruit Salad with Black-Eyed Peas

till they turn a bright red colour and plump up slightly. Remove and cool completely.

THE *PODI*

1 Ensure that the mixer jar is completely dry. My mum and grandma always keep the mixer jar in the sun before starting the prep for the *podi*, so that by the time the prep is done, the mixer jar is dry.

2 First grind the chillies into a coarse powder. Transfer to a large bowl.

3 Next, add all the remaining roasted ingredients – the dals, sesame seeds, peanuts and coconut – and use the pulse function of the mixer. Pulse 5–6 times for 10–20 seconds, opening the mixer jar and giving the contents a stir before the next pulse.

4 Remove this coarsely powdered *podi* to the bowl with the chilli powder.

5 Add the salt and stir well with a dry spoon to combine.

6 Once cool, transfer to airtight glass jars and keep in a cool, dry place.

Sesame seeds are rich in sesamin and sesamolin, which belong to a group of fibres called lignans. Lignans reduce cholesterol, prevent high blood pressure and increase the availability of vitamin E.

CALORIES (KCAL)	PROTEIN	FATS	CARBOHYDRATES	FIBRE
115	4.9	6.4	9.75	2.9

(per 2 tbsp)

Lemon Pepper Tahini

Tahini is the magic ingredient that gives hummus its characteristic flavour. It may not be easily available in all supermarkets but the good news is that it is very easy to make at home. Tahini adds a nutty creaminess to salad dressings.

MAKES
½ a cup of tahini

- ½ cup white sesame seeds, (unhulled)
- 1 tsp whole black peppercorns
- 2 lemons, zested
- ¾ tsp salt
- ½ tbsp lemon juice
- 2–3 tbsp of any neutral flavoured oil (light olive or ricebran)

1 Place a large frying pan over low heat and start toasting the sesame seeds.

2 The seeds will start popping. Keep tossing the sesame seeds in the pan till the popping sounds nearly stop.

3 Add the black peppercorns and lemon zest to the pan. Stir over low heat for 10–20 seconds.

4 Spread out in a dish to cool.

5 Transfer the toasted seeds, peppercorns and lemon zest to a mixer jar. Season with salt.

6 Blend till you get a powder consistency.

7 Pour in the lemon juice and 2 tbsp of oil. Bend for 30 seconds more till you get a smooth, pourable, thick, sauce-like consistency, adding the rest of the oil if required.

8 Save in an airtight container.

Using hulled white sesame seeds gives a lighter coloured and smoother tahini.

To make plain tahini, omit the pepper, lemon juice and zest and salt. Blend the toasted sesame seeds with the oil till you get a smooth paste.

Add 1 tbsp of lemon pepper tahini to savoury muffins and bakes to add to the nutritive value and for a sesame flavour.

You can also use this tahini to make a lemon-pepper hummus.

Thin the dressing by whisking in some yogurt. Dress steamed cauliflower and broccoli with this dressing to make a cruciferous salad.

Sesame seeds are rich in calcium, magnesium and iron as well as zinc, selenium and vitamin B1. The substance sesamin in sesame seeds is said to protect the liver from oxidative damage.

CALORIES (KCAL)	PROTEIN	FATS	CARBOHYDRATES	FIBRE
125	1.7	12	2.7	1.7

(per 1 tbsp)

Multipurpose Soya, Honey, Ginger Dressing

It's a dressing. It's a marinade. It's a dipping sauce. I absolutely adore multipurpose recipes like this one. It is versatile enough to warrant doubling or tripling the quantities and storing in your refrigerator for a quick Asian salad or as a dip for appetizers like summer spring rolls. I have even bottled this dressing and sold it at a local organic fair. Do remember to keep the fresh ginger overnight in the freezer before preparing the dish.

MAKES ¼ cup

- ½" piece fresh ginger, frozen
- 1 tbsp peanut oil
- 1 tsp sesame oil
- 3 tbsp dark soya sauce
- ½ tsp orange zest
- 1 tbsp honey
- 1 tbsp peanut butter
- ¼ tsp red chilli flakes
- 1 tbsp rice vinegar
- 1 tsp white sesame seeds

1 Scrape off the peel from the frozen ginger using the edge of a teaspoon. Grate the frozen ginger using a fine grater to get 1 teaspoonful.

2 Put all the ingredients, except the sesame seeds, into a small mixer jar or blender. Blend till the ingredients are well combined and you get a creamy dressing.

3 Stir in the sesame seeds.

4 Store in a clean, dry bottle in the refrigerator for up to 2–3 days.

Freezing the ginger before grating it yields very fine, almost paste-like grated ginger, allowing it to completely melt into the dressing. This is also the best way to infuse bold ginger flavour into your chai.

Use roasted, skinned peanuts instead of peanut butter and blend it into a butter first before adding the remaining ingredients to make the dressing.

Try and source organic oranges when you need orange zest.

Use this dressing to toss a noodle salad (rice noodles or egg noodles) with spirals of carrot, radish and zucchini, and shredded cabbage.

CALORIES (KCAL)	PROTEIN	FATS	CARBOHYDRATES	FIBRE
98	1.4	6.8	8.2	0.5

(per 1 tbsp)

Non-Dairy Cashew Cheesy Spread

This recipe needs overnight preparation or more but the end result is worth it, I promise. I need serious restraint not to consume the entire spread from the blender itself (with the excuse of tasting, of course!). It is a nod to all my vegan readers and friends, who are off dairy for a variety of reasons. It doesn't require any complex fermentation so I will refrain from calling it 'cheese' and just call it a 'cheesy' spread.

MAKES
approx. 150 ml

- 1 cup cashew halves
- 1½ tsp yellow mustard seeds
- ½ tsp garlic powder
- ½ tsp salt
- A pinch of sugar or a few drops of honey
- 2 tbsp rejuvelac or 1 tbsp white vinegar + 1 tbsp water (see cooking notes)

1 Soak the cashew nut halves and mustard seeds overnight in a bowl of hot water.

2 Drain using a fine-meshed sieve and transfer to a high-powered blender or one of those small bullet blenders used for smoothies.

3 Add the remaining ingredients and blend till you get a super creamy paste.

4 Scrape this out into an airtight jar and refrigerate.

Rejuvelac is a probiotic drink I make from sprouted wheat grains to drink first thing in the morning. It has a funky taste to it that gives this cashew spread a cheesy flavour. I understand that rejuvelac may not be an easy find in most kitchens, so go ahead and use a mix of vinegar and water instead.

I have used yellow mustard seeds because they infuse a zing into the cheesey spread minus the black flecks. They can easily be replaced with black mustard seeds.

Use this spread as a dip, or in sandwiches and on pizzas. You can also pair this spread with The Ultimate Superfood Burger (p. 4).

Cashews are rich in monounsaturated fats which are known for their heart-healthy characteristics. Eating a handful of nuts at least 4 times a week reduces the risk of developing cardiovascular diseases.

A typical 1 oz serving of cashews (16–18 pieces) provides an impressive 5 grams of protein for 155 calories. Keep a pre-portioned bag of roasted cashews handy for an evening snack.

CALORIES (KCAL)	PROTEIN	FATS	CARBOHYDRATES	FIBRE
51.6	1.8	4	2	0.3

(per 1 tbsp)

Mixed Seed Munch

My neighbour, Janaki, is a collector of all things beautiful. I was once travelling in her car when she pulled out a delicately etched silver box. Flipping open the lid, she tapped some flaxseeds in the palm of my hand. They were roasted to a crisp, pleasantly salted and a delight to munch on. This occurred a few years ago but the idea remained in my head ever since. My recipe for mixed seed munch is inspired from Janaki's roasted flaxseeds. This is a healthy-fat booster, a mouth-freshener and a boredom banisher, all rolled in one. Given Bengaluru's traffic, I make sure I always keep some in my car. (Talk about making the most of traffic jams!)

MAKES
¾ cup of seeds

- ¼ cup whole flaxseeds
- ¼ cup melon seeds
- 2 tbsp white sesame seeds
- 1 tbsp carom seeds (ajwain)
- 1 tbsp fennel seeds (saunf)
- 2 large betel leaves (magai paan), optional
- ½ tsp ghee
- ¼ tsp salt

1 Combine all the seeds in a microwave-safe glass baking tray. For this recipe, make sure the microwave is set at 60–70 per cent power (see cooking notes).

2 Microwave for 5 minutes, giving it a stir every 1–2 minutes to ensure that the seeds are not overly browned.

3 Finely chop the betel leaves and add them to the baking tray. Microwave for 2 minutes. The betel leaf bits will turn crisp.

4 Now mix in the ghee and salt, combining well with your fingertips to spread the seasoning uniformly. Microwave for another minute.

5 Remove from the microwave and allow to cool to room temperature.

6 Store in an airtight container. Munch on 1 tsp of the seed mix 2–3 times a day.

Use any other seeds you can find, such as pumpkin seeds, cucumber seeds, chia seeds, etc., in addition to these or as a replacement for any of the ones listed in the ingredients.

Flaxseeds contain higher levels of polyunsaturated fats including omega-3 polyunsaturated fat. These nutrients are more susceptible to heat damage, which is why they are best roasted at lower temperatures and durations. Ground flaxseeds contain more omega-3 fatty acids than salmon, 2 tbsp providing 1.6 grams.

Omega-3 from a vegan source is considered safer than a marine source which could have potential heavy metal contamination. Given that flaxseeds are rich in phytoestrogen, this superfood is useful for post-menopausal women as a natural source of oestrogen.

GARDENING TIP:

You can grow your own betel vine from a cutting (at least 18 cm). Remove all but the top two leaves and keep in a glass of water in the window sill, replacing with fresh water everyday. After a week or so, when new roots appear, transfer to a large pot or directly into soil. Partial sunlight and daily watering helps.

CALORIES (KCAL)	PROTEIN	FATS	CARBOHYDRATES	FIBRE
46	1.9	3.6	1.9	1.6

(per 1 tbsp)

Avocado Fruit Crèmes

I have tried this as a smoothie but it qualifies better as a dessert. Avocado makes it thick and creamy, while mangoes and figs make it naturally sweet. It satisfies the sweet tooth while packing a punch with its healthy fats and antioxidants.

SERVES 4

THE FRUITS
½ a large or 1 small ripe avocado
¼ lemon, juiced
3 ripe figs
1 cup mango cubes

THE OTHER INGREDIENTS
½ tsp vanilla extract
1 cup coconut water
4 ice cubes

THE AVOCADO AND FRUIT

1 Scoop out the flesh of the avocado. Chop it into chunks and sprinkle lemon juice. This will prevent it from turning brown.

2 Cut the figs into quarters.

3 Place the avocado, figs and mango in a freezer-safe container.

4 Freeze for 30 minutes to an hour.

TO PREPARE THE CRÈMES

1 Pour the coconut water and vanilla extract into a blender.

2 Add 4 ice cubes and the frozen avocado and fruit.

3 Blend till you get a smooth puree.

4 Divide between 4 small cups.

5 Serve chilled.

To make the crèmes richer use coconut milk instead of water. This is naturally sweet but mildly so. Sweeten with some honey or maple syrup if desired.

You can even have this as a smoothie bowl but it turns out quite filling as it is, so if you add more toppings like seeds or nuts, it may become too heavy to eat for breakfast.

A beauty tip for you! After scooping out the flesh of the avocado, the peel still has a thin layer of flesh sticking to it. Rub the flesh side of the peel all over your face and neck. Leave it for 15 minutes to dry. Wash with lukewarm water and pat dry for deliciously moisturized skin.

When avocados (rich in monounsaturated fats) are included in the diet, they not only improve the lipid profile in healthy individuals but also in those with mildly elevated cholesterol levels.

Figs are rich in dietary fibre (5 grams fibre per 100 grams of serving), contributing to the total required fibre intake in a day. Add ripe figs to smoothies, salads or eat as a snack.

CALORIES (KCAL)	PROTEIN	FATS	CARBOHYDRATES	FIBRE
148.9	1.9	8.9	15.9	5.0

(per serving)

Coconut Raw Mango Chutney

This spin on coconut chutney is a welcome break from the regular accompaniment to idlis and dosas. Make it when raw mangoes are in season.

SERVES 4

THE CHUTNEY

- 1 medium-sized green mango
- ½" piece of tamarind, without fibre and seeds
- ½ medium-sized fresh coconut, grated
- 4 green chillies, halved
- ¼ cup roasted gram
- ½" piece fresh ginger, grated
- ½ tsp salt

THE TEMPERING

- 2 tsp groundnut oil
- ½ tsp mustard seeds
- 1 tsp urad dal
- 1 dried red chilli
- 1 sprig fresh curry leaves
- A pinch of asafoetida powder (hing)

THE CHUTNEY

1. Peel the mango and chop the flesh.
2. Soak the tamarind in a small cup of hot water for 5–10 minutes.
3. Combine the mango, grated coconut, green chillies, fried gram, ginger and salt in a mixer jar.
4. Remove the soaked tamarind and add it to the blender.
5. Blend all the ingredients to make a smooth chutney.
6. Transfer to a bowl.

THE TEMPERING

1. Heat the oil in a small pan or a tempering ladle.
2. Add all the ingredients for the tempering in the order mentioned.
3. When the mustard seeds splutter and the dal turns golden-brown, pour the contents of the pan over the chutney.
4. Keep refrigerated till ready to serve.

You can add a piece of ripe avocado to get an even creamier texture.

Use 1 tbsp of sour yogurt as a substitute for tamarind.

Don't skimp on the tempering. The crunch from the mustard seeds and urad dal is the highlight of the chutney.

Raw mangoes lighten up the chutney by replacing part of the coconut. Roasted gram is rich in heart-healthy mono and polyunsaturated fats. When eating rice-dominant breakfasts such as dosas and idlis, coconut with its extremely low glycaemic index of just 1, helps balance the glycaemic index of the meal.

CALORIES (KCAL)	PROTEIN	FATS	CARBOHYDRATES	FIBRE
14.5	0.3	0.9	1.4	0.4

(per serving)

Soya Wasabi Peanuts

Minimal ingredients and a microwave oven work together to give you the perfect crunchy snack to stock up on before the weekend begins. I buy a kilo of the best peanuts from our local supplier and prepare a big jar of these soya wasabi peanuts as well as, sometimes, sriracha peanuts. These also make great party appetizers with little effort from your end.

MAKES
about 2 cups of peanuts

2 cups raw peanuts
2 tsp groundnut oil
2 tsp wasabi paste
1 tbsp dark soya sauce
½ tsp red chilli powder

1 Place the peanuts in a glass baking tray and microwave on 80 per cent power setting for 3 minutes.

2 Meanwhile, whisk the oil, wasabi paste, soya sauce and chilli powder in a small bowl to get a smooth mixture.

3 Sprinkle this spice mix over the peanuts and toss them well.

4 Microwave for another 2–3 minutes, giving them a stir once every minute. The peanuts should be quite dry by this time. They will crisp up further on cooling.

5 Remove and cool to room temperature before storing in airtight containers.

Instead of soya and wasabi, you can use flavours like honey and chilli powder, lemon zest and thyme or even mint and turmeric to coat the peanuts.

Other nuts like almonds, cashews and hazelnuts can also be treated in the same way. Roasting times may vary depending on the size of the nut.

Several studies have shown that nutrients found in peanuts, including folic acid, phytosterols, phytic acid (inositol hexaphosphate) and resveratrol have anti-cancer effects, especially on colon cancer.

Roasted peanuts have as much antioxidants as some of the berries.

CALORIES (KCAL)	PROTEIN	FATS	CARBOHYDRATES	FIBRE
221	9.4	19.1	6.7	3.1

(per ¼ cup)

Peanut Satay Sauce

What momos, spring rolls, Vietnamese summer rolls and shumai need is a killer dipping sauce. This satay sauce with the heartiness of peanuts provides just that. It also makes the perfect accompaniment to dip crudités or chunks of roasted vegetables – making a great party appetizer!

MAKES 2 cups

- 1 cup unsalted peanuts, roasted
- 6 tbsp dark soya sauce
- 3 tbsp grated jaggery
- 1 tsp lemon zest
- 6 tbsp lemon juice
- 1½ tsp grated fresh ginger
- 1 tbsp tamarind paste
- 3 tbsp peanut oil
- 1 tbsp red chilli powder

1 Mix all the ingredients in the small jar of the mixer and grind to a fine paste.

2 Add ¾ cup of water and run the mixer for a bit longer, till you get a smooth sauce.

3 Remove into a small serving bowl.

Use coconut milk instead of water to prepare a smaller batch or for one-time use.

Peanuts are rich in monounsaturated fats, which are a part of a heart-healthy, Mediterranean diet. It also contains vitamin E, folic acid, niacin and important trace minerals. Peanuts contain the antioxidant reservatrol, also found in red grapes and red wine. People consuming nuts at least 4 times a week showed a 37 per cent reduced risk of coronary heart disease compared to those who never or seldom ate nuts.

Tamarind is a good source of calcium and iron.

CALORIES (KCAL)	PROTEIN	FATS	CARBOHYDRATES	FIBRE
181	4.8	12.1	15.9	1.8

(per ¼ cup)

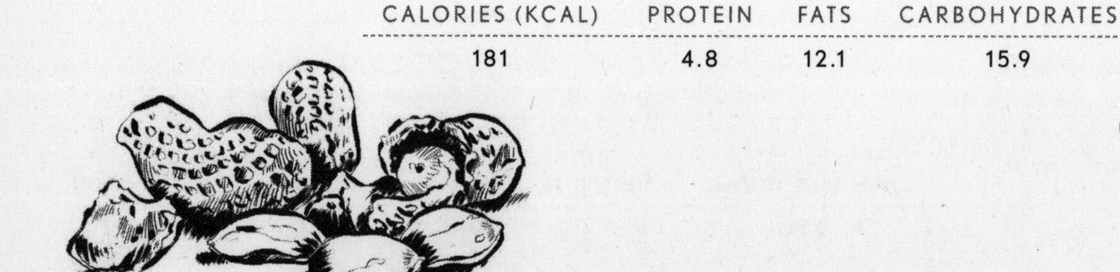

Citrus and Olive Oil Dressing

There's something about the combination of oranges and extra-virgin olive oil that adds a dollop of sunshine to every salad that it dresses. Fresh orange juice and orange zest give it the bright flavours to elevate any bowl of food, be it pasta, veggies or beans. This recipe makes enough dressing to go over 4–5 salads.

MAKES
A little over 1 cup of dressing

- ½ cup extra-virgin olive oil
- 2½ tbsp apple cider vinegar
- ½ cup orange juice, freshly squeezed
- Zest of 2 oranges
- 1 tsp salt
- 2 tbsp honey

1 Mix all the ingredients in a blender till you get a smooth and creamy dressing.

2 Keep refrigerated for up to a week or 10 days. Shake well before use.

Buy and store extra-virgin olive oil in dark-coloured, smaller sized bottles, as the oil turns rancid when exposed to heat and light. Even though rich in monounsaturated fats, olive oil is quite heat resistant and stable compared to other polyunsaturated fats. Pour out a smaller quantity in a bottle to keep handy and store the rest in a cool, dry place so that the heat from the cooking range does not affect the whole bottle.

Extra-virgin olive oil has anti-inflammatory properties, which reduce the risk of cardiovascular disease in doses as low as 1 tbsp per day. This provides 13 per cent of the daily requirement of vitamin E, a potent antioxidant. Extra-virgin olive oil helps improve blood sugar regulation and insulin levels.

Adding this olive oil dressing to a grain or potato-based salad reduces the glycaemic index of the entire dish, leading to slow and gradual rise of blood sugar.

CALORIES (KCAL)	PROTEIN	FATS	CARBOHYDRATES	FIBRE
118.6	-	11.7	4.4	-

(per 2 tbsp)

Avocado, Coconut Chips and Whole Bengal Gram Salad

Perfectly ripened avocados can be put to use in many a recipe, from guacamole to green smoothies. Making a salad with the protein-rich Bengal gram (kala chana) and coconut chips gives a boost of healthy fats to your meal while keeping you feeling full for a good 3–4 hours. I love the colour contrast and sweet-tartness that the plums bring to the salad.

SERVES 2

2 handfuls fresh salad greens
¾ cup Bengal gram (kala chana), cooked
1 large ripe avocado
½ lemon, juiced
2 ripe plums
¼ cup coconut chips
1 tbsp extra-virgin olive oil

THE GARNISH

Pink salt or any coarse salt
¼ tsp sumac
¼ tsp freshly ground black pepper

1 Start by layering two salad plates with a handful of salad greens each.

2 Divide the kala chana between the two plates.

3 Cut the avocado in half by running a sharp knife around its length. Loosen the seed and discard. Using the edge of a spoon, scoop out the flesh and cut into bite-sized chunks, coating it in lemon juice immediately to prevent browning.

4 Top the kala chana with avocado chunks.

5 Chop the plums into bite-sized pieces and layer on top of both salads.

6 Sprinkle coconut chips all over.

7 Drizzle extra-virgin olive oil over the salads.

8 Grind the coarse salt and black pepper and sprinkle some sumac over the salad.

9 Serve immediately.

See photograph 28 of colour insert.

If plums are not in season, use dried cranberries for sweetness and colour.

Instead of coconut chips you can slice up a dried coconut (copra) and toss in a heavy bottomed pan for 5–6 minutes over low heat, till crisp.

Check the general cooking notes section on tips to ripen avocados.

Half an avocado provides 7 per cent of the daily vitamin E requirement and 4.6 grams of dietary fibre. Avocados are rich in monounsaturated fats that are known to reverse insulin resistance and stabilize blood sugar levels, making it an excellent ingredient to include in a diabetic's diet.

CALORIES (KCAL)	PROTEIN	FATS	CARBOHYDRATES	FIBRE
367.8	5.7	29.9	21.6	10.5

(per serving)

Niger Seed Chutney

I was introduced to niger seeds on my trip to Sikkim. These seeds look like a shinier black version of cumin seeds. I was surprised when the shopkeeper told me that they are closer to sesame seeds in terms of flavour. Not being one to pass over a good ingredient when I spot it, I got a packet back with me to Bengaluru, with instructions on how to use it. Imagine my surprise when my housekeeper told me that this seed is quite popular in Karnataka cuisine and it is called *gurellu* in Kannada. The recipe for this chutney is adapted from the one the shopkeeper in Sikkim shared with me.

SERVES 4

2 tbsp niger seeds (ramtil)
½ tsp oil
2 dried red chillies
2 cloves garlic
¼ tsp rock salt

1 Pick out and discard any stones or twigs in the niger seeds.

2 Put the oil in a small frying pan over low to moderate heat.

3 Add the niger seeds, red chillies and garlic. Slow roast for 8–10 minutes. Niger seeds don't pop as much as sesame seeds but keep your ears open for a light crackle.

4 At this point remove the ingredients on to a plate and cool.

5 You can either grind them coarsely along with the salt in a mixer jar using the pulse function or pound it in a wide mortar-pestle.

6 Niger seeds have a thick husk, which takes time to break down in a mortar-pestle.

TO SERVE

1 Serve with a simple meal of dal, rice and subzi (as in Sikkimese cuisine).

2 Eat the chutney with jowar rotis (as in North Karnataka).

3 It also makes a flavoursome *podi* to have with idlis and dosas.

It is interesting to note that niger seeds are primarily grown for their oil. The seed is more popular as bird feed. The Indian names for niger seeds are ramtil *in Hindi,* gurellu uchellu *in Kannada,* filunge/ramtil/jhuse til *in Nepalese and in Sikkim, and* payellu/uchellu *in Tamil.*

Niger seeds are one of the richest sources of iron (56 mg of iron per 100 grams), which is double the daily requirement for adults. Having a tbsp of this chutney along with a meal contributes significantly to the iron requirement for a day.

CALORIES (KCAL)	PROTEIN	FATS	CARBOHYDRATES	FIBRE
33.9	1.4	2.5	1.6	0.6

(per serving)

Spiced Coconut Oil Dressing

This is similar to a South Indian tadka or tempering, but minus the leaves and whole spices that most people don't like to bite into. The coconut oil carries all the flavours from the spices. In winters, warm a spoon or two of this dressing in a small ladle to liquefy it before using.

MAKES
½ cup of dressing

½ cup virgin coconut oil
5 dried red chillies
4 sprigs fresh curry leaves
1" piece fresh ginger, sliced
1 tsp whole black peppercorns
1 tsp cumin seeds
¼ tsp fenugreek seeds

1 Heat the oil in a small pan over moderate heat.

2 Add all the ingredients and stir through. Allow the chillies and ginger to crisp up. The curry leaves will crackle and turn a dark green.

3 Reduce the heat to low and allow the ingredients to steep in the oil for 5–7 minutes.

4 Keep aside in a cool, dry place.

5 Once the oil reaches room temperature, strain the spiced dressing through a dry strainer into a clean glass jar.

6 Discard the fried spices.

TO SERVE

1 Toss any grain or vegetable salad in this oil with a pinch of salt and a squeeze of lemon juice. A garnish of fresh coconut will add to the flavour.

Steamed vegetables such as potato, carrot, beans and cabbage can also be tossed in this oil with salt, pepper and fresh coconut.

Instead of discarding the spices, grind one spoon of the spices and herbs with enough coconut and salt to make a spicy coconut chutney.

Over 50 per cent of the fats in coconut oil are medium chain fatty acids such as lauric acid, a saturated fat that is known for its anti-bacterial and anti-fungal properties, which is the reason that coconut oil, despite being a saturated fat, is widely known for its health benefits.

Curry leaves are rich in carotene and calcium. Dry-roast curry leaves along with the spices and make a powder to serve with rice or as an accompaniment to South Indian breakfasts.

CALORIES (KCAL)	PROTEIN	FATS	CARBOHYDRATES	FIBRE
124	0.1	13.6	0.5	0.3

(per 1 tbsp)

The After-Dinner Bark

It is unrealistic to expect a sweet tooth to take premature retirement. But it can be trained to accept healthier alternatives like this one. Chocolate, nuts, dried fruit, coconut and sesame seeds come together in every bite of this after-dinner bark. Make a big batch and store in an air-tight container in the refrigerator.

MAKES 16 pieces

- ¼ cup almonds
- ¼ cup cashews
- 1 cup semi-sweet chocolate chips
- 5–6 drops orange oil (see cooking notes below)
- ¼ cup dried cranberries
- ¼ cup coconut chips
- 1 tsp white sesame seeds

1 Toast the almonds and cashews for 3 minutes on high in the microwave, giving it a stir every 45 seconds or so. Remove and chop roughly. Allow to cool and crisp up.

2 Fill a medium-sized pan with roughly 2" of water and bring it to a boil over high heat.

3 Once the water is boiling, reduce the heat and place a bowl on top of the pan, such that the bottom of the bowl does not touch the water's surface.

4 Place the chocolate chips in the bowl and allow them to melt over the simmering water in the pan below.

5 Using a silicone spatula, keep stirring the chocolate around to enable melting.

6 Remove the bowl with the melted chocolate from the pan of water and vigorously stir in circles using the silicon spatula till chocolate is glossy. Add the orange oil and combine well.

7 Add the nuts, cranberries and coconut chips and stir to combine.

8 Line a small baking tray with parchment paper. Transfer the chocolate mixture over the paper.

9 Smoothen out to a ½"-thick bark using the spatula.

10 Sprinkle sesame seeds all over and press down with the spatula.

11 Place this tray in the freezer for 10 minutes.

12 Once it has set, break into pieces of desired sizes. Save in an airtight box in the refrigerator.

Orange oil is available in shops selling baking supplies. If you cannot find it, use orange extract or vanilla extract.

If you don't have chocolate chips, use the best dark chocolate bar you can find.

Instead of coconut chips, use thinly sliced dried coconut. Toast it lightly in the microwave or on the stovetop and add to melted chocolate.

Use thick parchment paper so that the bark can be easily removed. Thin baking paper tends to stick to the chocolate bark, making it difficult to peel off. Otherwise, brush a baking tray lightly with 2 drops of oil and transfer the chocolate mixture over this.

This bark provides healthy fats from nuts and coconut, and antioxidants from dark chocolate. Eating a piece of bark as a post-dinner treat ensures you get a serving of healthy fats.

CALORIES (KCAL)	PROTEIN	FATS	CARBOHYDRATES	FIBRE
72.0	0.8	4.9	7.2	1.2

(per piece)

Sample Menu Plan for a Week

	BREAKFAST	LUNCH/ LUNCH BOX	DINNER
MONDAY	Overnight oats with sautéed apples	Drumstick curry; Roti; Indian gooseberry, carrot and pomegranate in yogurt (Amla, gajar and anar in raita)	Broken wheat and mixed-sprout khichdi with fried garlic; Yogurt
TUESDAY	No-cook red rice poha with kachumber	Mixed lentils with Malabar Spinach; Not your usual kachumber; Roti	Curried millets with tofu crumble
WEDNESDAY	Green paneer scramble (bhurji); Whole-wheat bread	Potato lettuce salad with chilli garlic dressing, wrapped in rotis	Medley of gourds in coconut milk; Cooked millets
THURSDAY	Green pancakes (chila)	Cauliflower with chickpeas, wrapped in rotis or tortillas	Paneer in banana leaf parcels (paneer paturi); Rice; Roasted pineapple chilli chutney
FRIDAY	Little millet tomato 'rice'	Purple cabbage with leafy greens (*thoran*); Red rice; Medley of gourds in coconut milk	The ultimate superfood burger; Baked tapioca chips
SATURDAY	Banana and buckwheat pancakes	Brown rice with spinach and chickpeas; Green apple rasam	My glorious panzanella salad; Baked zucchini pasta; The after-dinner bark
SUNDAY	Baked egg cups; Green rice-flour dumplings; Tulsi *thogayal*	Savoury loaf; The happy salad; Roasted fruit salad with honey cream and mint	Curried moth bean sprouts (matki)

Dietary Index

SUPERFOOD RECIPES

Superfood recipes have a higher concentration of vitamins, minerals and antioxidants.

VEGAN RECIPES

Vegan recipes are free from animal products like milk, yogurt, cheese, ghee and honey. There are some more recipes in the book which can be made vegan by replacing ghee with oil and omitting cheese.

GLUTEN-FREE RECIPES

Gluten-free recipes are free from gluten-containing grains and flours as well as soya sauce.

DIABETIC-FRIENDLY RECIPES

Diabetic-friendly recipes contain complex carbohydrates, providing more protein and higher fibre. These recipes are lower in glycemic index due to the combination of ingredients used, causing a gradual rise in blood sugar after the meal, making it suitable for diabetics.

Recipe Index

H

N

O

Q

R

Acknowledgements

A project like this is never undertaken alone, and I could never have done this without the support of several members of my family and my friends. While I'm trying my best to not make this sound like an Oscar acceptance speech, I do have a lot of people to express my gratitude to.

First, I would like to thank my parents. Appa was a foodie in the real sense of the word and would eat a simple meal with much gusto. He would have been very proud to see my first cookbook. Amma has always been my quiet supporter and one word of praise from her gives me the strength to do more.

I'm grateful to my grandparents for always being generous with their blessings.

I must make a special mention of Geetha Chithi, my aunt and favourite cook in the family. My childhood would not have been the same without her bread rolls, beetroot halva and the pressure-cooker cakes. I'm grateful for her inspiration in my early years of cooking.

A big thank you goes out to my husband, who has always encouraged me to follow my dreams. His willingness to try any dish I come up with has been a big contributor to my creativity in the kitchen. His asking me, 'So what's the status of the book?' every couple of days made me stay focused on my goal.

Thank you, my darling son, for always giving me constructive feedback and funny one liners. Always the connoisseur of good food, he also did his best not to lay his hands on the food before it had been photographed. Thank you to my sister and A & A, my baby niece and nephew. Your cute antics on video chat always cheered me up at the end of a very hectic day.

I am also grateful to my friends, who have always loved my cooking, making me believe in myself. Nandini and Ajit, thank you for pushing me to start the salad workshops and to write a book featuring my salads; Bharath and Vijay, thank you for just hanging out with me and helping me unwind after a stressful week; Lakshmi, thank you for talking to me every single day (it can be very lonely working all by yourself).

Chef Manu Chandra, thanks for going through the plan for this book and giving your invaluable inputs, despite your busy schedule. Your validation gave me the confidence to soldier on.

To the friends who have been a part of my blogging journey over the last 12 years, thank you for keeping my love for cooking and blogging burning bright.

A huge thank you to my neighbours who, despite their busy schedules, agreed to test the recipes from the book.

My wonderful blog readers, thank you for sticking by me for the last 12 years and giving me your love and support, and egging me on to hone my skills.

My Twitter friends, thanks for being an endless source of inspiration, constructive criticism and cheering.

I would also like to thank the team at HealthifyMe, who helped me with the nutritional labels for all the recipes, thereby freeing up my time to focus on the edits. Thanks must also go to Farrukh, for generously allowing me to borrow some props for the shoot.

Last, but not the least, I would like to thank my editor, Prerna Vohra, who kick-started this book with her one email in 2015. Her calm demeanour was the perfect balance to my panic modes, and it was amazing how aligned our choices were with respect to the content, the fonts, layouts and everything else. For a first-time author, I could not have asked for a better person to guide me through this process.

Nandita Iyer is a medical doctor with a specialization in nutrition. Having started her career in the health insurance and healthcare advertising industry, she transitioned into a full-time nutrition expert and a seasoned columnist. She has written on nutrition, health and food for over a decade, and her articles have appeared in *Men's Health*, BBC Good Food, *Femina*, *Mint*, *The Hindu* and BuzzFeed, among others. As the author of the popular food blog *Saffron Trail*, she has been featured in *Vogue*, *Femina*, Fox Life, *India Today*, *Times of India* and others. She also conducts healthy cooking workshops for individuals and companies. When she is not busy multitasking at work, her favourite ways to de-stress are singing, pulling out weeds in her garden and watching *Downton Abbey*.

Nandita lives in Bengaluru with her ultra-marathoner husband, nine-year-old son and enough books to fill several libraries. You can connect with her on Twitter @saffrontrail or Facebook.com/saffrontrail. If you try any of the recipes from this book, share it with her on Instagram using the hashtag #saffrontrail. You can also visit her website, saffrontrail.com, and sign up for the newsletter.